VÉRONIQUE TADJO was born in Paris and grew up in Abidjan, Côte d'Ivoire. She has a degree from Abidjan University and a doctorate degree in African American Literature and Civilization from the Sorbonne. She has lectured at Abidjan University. Tadjo's work includes two collections of poems, *Latérite* (Hatier, 1984), which won a literary award, and *A mi-chemin* (L'Harmattan, 2000); three novels, *Le Royaume Aveugle* (L'Harmattan, 1992), *A Vol d'Oiseau* (Nathan, 1991 and L'Harmattan, 1992) and *Champs de Bataille et d'Amour* (Présence Africaine/Nouvelles Editions Ivoiriennes, 1999). She has written and illustrated several children's books and has edited a short anthology of African poetry, *Talking Drums* (A & C Black, 2000). She has facilitated workshops on writing and illustrating children's books in several countries. The English edition of *A Vol d'Oiseau*, *As the Crow Flies*, was published in the African Writers Series in 2001.

VÉRONIQUE WAKERLEY was born in Britain and educated in Britain, France and Zimbabwe, and has a Master of Arts from Exeter University and a doctorate in French from the University of London. She lectures in French at the University of Zimbabwe and is particularly interested in the literature of the first part of the twentieth century. She also teaches literary and general translation both at undergraduate level and to postgraduates studying for a Diploma in Translation. In the context of her academic work, she has become engaged in an ongoing project to promote works of Francophone literature through translation into English, and the first book in the series, *Fools, Thieves and Other Dreamers*, was published by Weaver Press in 2001. A second collection of stories by Francophone women writers, including one by Véronique Tadjo, is to be published by Weaver Press.

VÉRONIQUE TADJO

THE SHADOW OF IMANA
Travels in the heart of Rwanda

Translated by Véronique Wakerley

Heinemann

Heinemann Educational Publishers
Halley Court, Jordan Hill, Oxford OX2 8EJ
A part of Harcourt Education Limited

Heinemann: A Division of Reed Publishing (USA) Inc.
361 Hanover Street, Portsmouth, NH 03801-3912, USA

Heinemann Publishers (Pty) Limited
PO Box 781940, Sandton 2146, Johannesburg, South Africa

OXFORD MELBOURNE AUCKLAND
JOHANNESBURG BLANTYRE GABORONE
IBADAN PORTSMOUTH (NH) USA CHICAGO

First published by Heinemann Educational Publishers in 2002

Available in Zimbabwe from Weaver Press

British Library Cataloguing in Publication Data
A catalogue record for this book is available from the British Library.

Author photograph by Howard Phillips
Cover photograph by Catherine Millet

Printed and bound in Great Britain by
Cox and Wyman Ltd, Reading, Berkshire

ISBN 0 435 91015 9

02 03 04 05 06 07 08 8 7 6 5 4 3 2 1

Contents

To all of those who are gone
But who remain forever in our hearts

The First Journey

It had long been my dream to go to Rwanda. No, 'dream' is not the right word. I had long felt a need to exorcise Rwanda. To go to that place where those images we had seen on television had been filmed, images that had flashed across the world and had left an indelible horror in every heart. I did not want Rwanda to remain forever a nightmare, a primal fear.

I was starting from a particular premise: what had happened there concerned us all. It was not just one nation lost in the dark heart of Africa that was affected. To forget Rwanda after the sound and the fury was like being blind in one eye, voiceless, handicapped. It was to walk in darkness, feeling your way with outstretched arms to avoid colliding with the future.

Of course, I did not consciously think this. I just wanted to go to Rwanda because I needed to.

Occasionally, someone will reveal a secret to you that you have not asked to know. Then you are crushed under a burden of knowledge too heavy to bear. I could no longer keep Rwanda buried inside me. I needed to lance the abscess, lay bare the wound and bandage it. I am not a doctor, but I could still try to administer first aid to myself.

As I had been invited to South Africa for a conference a few days before my trip to Rwanda, I told myself that it was a good jumping-off point. Post-apartheid South Africa might perhaps be able to offer some answers to my questions, especially in relation to the problem of reconciliation on a national scale. Furthermore, my first contact with this country would lead to other trips, I was sure. South Africa forms part of our collective memory.

Nevertheless, I did not expect to have my first encounter with Rwanda while I was in South Africa.

DURBAN, SOUTH AFRICA

A beach-side parking lot

Life is filled with random events that cannot be explained. The man was guarding the cars in the parking lot where we had left our vehicle.

He arrived eight months ago by way of Zaïre. He made the journey on foot from Rwanda. He lives in a township, in a small room he shares with others, who, like him, have ended up here.

He fled to the very edge of the sea.

◆

I only saw his eyes. They were covered in an opaque film. Nothing could be read in his deep, unfathomable gaze. He seemed unable to capture life in those pupils, to recognise the sun, the sky, the city. His eyes were those of a prisoner, eyes blinded by darkness and emptiness.

For a fraction of a second I was overcome by a feeling of dizziness. Behind us, the sea thundered and the waves broke on the shore. Our skin was damp from the sea spray.

The man had moved his lips. I heard him ask what I was going to do there in his country, Rwanda.

JOHANNESBURG

I have not been able to get a direct flight from Johannesburg to Kigali. Going via Nairobi would have cost me a day or two. I have chosen to go Johannesburg–Paris–Brussels–Kigali in a single journey. The ground staff at the check-in counter tells me I cannot check my case through beyond Paris. The computer (?).

The journey is smooth but I do not manage to sleep. I look out of the aircraft window at the black sky peppered with stars. I think of my mother. I cannot believe that she is gone. I feel her close to me. I feel her still present beside me. I have the impression that she is with me, that she is holding my hand on this journey in which I am bound to meet death.

PARIS–BRUSSELS

No problems. But when I get there, I have to run. I must collect my baggage, then check in for Kigali in less than an hour. The airport is teeming. I have difficulty in getting my bearings. My bag does not appear. I should have known this would happen. I have only half an hour left. I go to the passenger services desk. I am beside myself, I am going to miss my plane. 'Report your loss at Kigali!' I have no time to argue the matter. The departure gate is a long way away. I must not miss this flight.

SABENA FLIGHT 565

At last, I am here, finally in my seat. I suppose it could have been worse. I have not taken out baggage insurance as I was advised to do before my departure.

Fortunately, in my hand luggage, I have my toilet bag, all my documents and valuables. No change of clothes. I will have to work out what to do when I get there.

The plane is almost empty. I have a row of seats to myself.

A group of passengers, Rwandans, are laughing a lot. They have not stopped talking since take-off. The young woman in their party is tall and beautiful, her laughter infectious. I do not yet know that she will become a friend. The men are in their forties and are elegantly dressed, no doubt high-ranking civil servants or administrators in some international organisation.

There are some nuns dressed in blue making quiet conversation.

A fairly mature couple travelling with their baby cause a great fuss when the meal is served because the baby's bottle is not brought on time. Belgians? French?

They are probably not going as far as Kigali. The plane has a stop-over at Nairobi.

The couple ask the Rwandans to lower their voices, as the baby has just gone to sleep.

I read the paper. The tourists murdered in Uganda are still making headline news. This time, it is a background article. The journalist stresses that everywhere in the world there are risks attached to travelling.

Eight foreigners, including an American couple, have been murdered in the Ugandan jungle by, according to informed sources, Hutu rebels. Despite the steep terrain and the insects, the tourists had come in the hope of seeing some gorillas.

The journalist wants to know who is to blame, starting with the travel agency and going right on up to the government and political authorities in Uganda who neglected to inform the tourists of the risks they were running.

In my case though, no one could claim that I have not been duly warned. At the end of the article, the journalist gives a list of high-risk countries: Angola, Rwanda, Burundi, both Congos, Sierra Leone, Guinea Bissau, Sudan, as well as Iran, Iraq, Afghanistan, Bosnia and Serbia.

I tell myself that you can get yourself killed in many other places. In New York, Johannesburg, Durban, Lagos, Nairobi or Abidjan.

I wonder suddenly if my Ivorian nationality would be an advantage or a death sentence.

I am weary.

I cannot manage to sleep. My mind is spinning. I put on the headphones and try to watch the film. But I cannot bring myself to be interested in this Hollywood romance. I read for a while.

We begin the descent to Kigali. I have no entry visa. A letter of invitation should suffice. I count my dollars. I have been advised to bring some; apparently they are more useful than French francs. I think of my suitcase. What are my chances of getting it back? I try to remember everything that it contains.

On arrival, I must pass through Immigration. I am ushered into a small room. Several people are waiting there. When my turn comes, the officer speaks to me in English. He wants to know why I have come to Rwanda. He smiles and speaks to me courteously. He seems pleased that I can express myself in English. I shall find this language useful several times during my stay in Rwanda. The English-speaking Rwandans come from Uganda or from Tanzania where they were living in exile for several decades. The high-ranking officers in the RPF, the army that liberated the country, are mainly of Ugandan origin. They are the people in charge today.

The officer issues me with a visa on a loose sheet of paper. But I shall still need to go to the Ministry of National Security to get my passport back as they decide to keep it.

8

KIGALI

From a distance, the city seems to have forgotten everything, digested everything, swallowed everything. The streets are full of people. The flow of cars is never-ending. Everyone wants to make a place for themselves, begin everything all over again.

To stroll casually in the streets and watch life go by. To buy bananas from a stall, laugh with the kids, chat with someone in the street, wait at a red light for the little green man to appear, buy the newspaper, drink a Coke at a kiosk, live in Kigali as if the past were only a bad memory. The faces look familiar to me. Everything is so similar to my own home that it breaks my heart.

Kigali in peacetime is a very calm Kigali.

Night falls. The darkness is dense. Dots of light decorate the hills like candles on a Christmas tree. Car headlights pierce the darkness in the distance. Everything is in slow motion, calmed by the ending of the day. The street lamps throw off a dull glare. The air is cool, the ground warm.

Near a building, beneath the sleeping trees, rows of tables, upturned chairs await the approaching dawn. In the surrounding houses, everything seems to be going along quite normally. The noise from television sets slips along the avenues. There are sounds of frying, water running, a car starting, a neighbour calling to her child. Silhouettes stand out against the windows, like a Chinese shadow show behind closed curtains. The night is like every other night.

The moon is a perfect half-circle. The stars keep their painful secrets to themselves. Nothing can pierce the impenetrable darkness.

We have to remember that time of endless night, return to that time of great terror, the time when humans, face to face with their destiny, had not yet discovered their humanity. Their steps were guided by obscure fears. We must remember the physical fear of the Other.

Are your fears more terrifying than mine? Do you fall deeper into your abyss than I into mine? What sacrifice would you be willing to make to preserve your humanity?

Are you prepared for this incredible encounter with death distorted by cruelty?

For one day we must stop in our tracks to look ourselves in the face, set off in search of our own fears buried beneath apparent serenity.

◆

May my eyes see, may my ears hear, may my mouth speak. I am not afraid of knowing. But may my mind never ever lose sight of what must grow within us: hope and respect for life.

Yes, let us look at life as it flows along: daily gestures, ordinary words. Everyday life as it really is.

Just as in some of the Pacific Isles, people return to settle at the foot of an extinct volcano to till the fertile soil, Kigali is shedding its past and donning the raiment of a new existence.

People's politeness, the surprise in their eyes when they see you pass by, their hearty laughter, leave you feeling bereft of your points of reference. In the face of so much tranquillity, how can you conceive of the violence that filled these very streets, took these very same meandering paths, invaded this very space?

A lot of time is needed to accept that trees planted in this land of sorrows have been able to bear fruit.

Traces of the war are rare in the town but people's memories are teeming with poisoned images. The vast majority of people carry their pain silently in their souls and find the unbelievable strength to live daily life as it begins again; watches have had their time set right, calendars have been hung up on the walls again, books picked up from the dust, photographs have been found and stuck back into the album, brought out of the past and oblivion. Gestures of no importance, but whose value is so great that they impose respect on every generation.

The truth is revealed in people's eyes. Words have so little value. You need to get under people's skins. See what is inside.

Evil changes its tactics and chooses different battlefields. It emerges wherever we have lowered our guard.

NYAMATA CHURCH

Site of genocide.

Plus or minus 35,000 dead.

A woman bound hand and foot.

Mukandori. Aged twenty-five. Exhumed in 1997.

Home: the town of Nyamata.

Married.

Any children?

Her wrists are bound, and tied to her ankles. Her legs are spread wide apart. Her body is lying on its side. She looks like an enormous fossilised foetus. She has been laid on a dirty blanket, in front of carefully lined up skulls and bones scattered on a mat.

She has been raped. A pickaxe has been forced into her vagina. She died from a machete blow to the nape of her neck. You can see the groove left by the impact. She still has a blanket over her shoulders but the material is now encrusted into the skin.

She is there as an example, exhumed from the ditch where she had fallen with the other bodies. On show so that no one can forget. A mummified victim of genocide. Remnants of hair are still attached to her skull.

WEAPONS

Grenades, rifles, hammers, spiked clubs, axes, machetes, hoes. The machetes came from France and China.

Mines in the surrounding countryside.

To wipe out all evidence, the skulls could be burnt.

They say, too, that when the United Nations forces arrived, the soldiers removed the bodies.

Only those bodies that could eventually be identified were buried in accordance with the rites. All the others are there, to bear witness, and will have no burial. They are nothing but bones.

Those blackened skulls are those which were found in latrines or buried in the earth. Those white ones were found in the open, among the tall grasses.

But these dead are screaming still. The chaos remains palpable. The events are too recent. This is not a memorial but death laid bare, exposed in all its rawness.

The horror of the sullied earth and of time laying down layers of dust in its passage. The bones of the skeleton-corpses are disintegrating before our very eyes. The stench infects our nostrils and settles inside our lungs, contaminates our flesh, infiltrates our brains. Even later on, far away, this smell will linger in our bodies and our minds.

Sheaves of dried flowers decorate the bones.

Seen through the holes left by the grenades in the walls of the church: piles of bones, skulls, muddy clothes, scattered, broken objects, upturned furniture.

◆

It was on 15 April 1994 between 7.30 in the morning and 2 o'clock in the afternoon that the massacre unfolded at

Nyamata. Several thousand people had taken refuge in the church and its outbuildings. There were also people occupying the offices of the priest and the administration. Many were sleeping under the stars in the courtyard, all huddled up together.

Not far from there, some people were sheltering in a maternity ward among the pregnant women and new-borns.

The authorities had asked the people to gather together: 'Assemble in the churches and public places, we will protect you.'

At the end of the war, it was the survivors who retrieved the skeletons and the scattered bones.

It was all done in a great hurry. They look like things destined for the scrapyard. Skulls are piled on top of each other, torn and mouldy clothes mingle with the scarcely recognisable remains.

Driver ants criss-cross the red earth. What do they remember of the genocide?

The Belgian priest was no longer there when the massacre took place.

The little town is surrounded by marshes. Survivors hid there until 14 May, when the RPF, the liberation army, arrived. They slept in the water, lived in the water. Many of them died among the papyrus.

◆

On the other side of the fence, a woman is watching us. I smile at her. She waves at me.

The guide invites me to come and write in the register.

I am number 7317.

I write my surname and my first name.

My address in Rwanda.

My address abroad.

13

In the column headed 'remarks', I have difficulty in gathering my thoughts. I jot down a phrase about the horror of genocide.

Before getting into the vehicle which brought us here, I wonder if I should give the guide some money. Yes.

NTARAMA CHURCH

Site of genocide.

Plus or minus 5,000 dead.

White-haired and serene, the little old man has a quizzical look. He is observing the visitors, weighing them up, studying them closely, stripping them of their masks. He can categorise them straight away: those who will avert their gaze from the spectacle of death laid out before them, those who will be shocked, those who will weep, those who will remain silent, those who will ask questions, pen in hand, those who will seek to rationalise, to understand, those who will give him money and those who will not dare, those who will write: 'Never again!'

He knows who you are immediately, whether you are afraid of death. And when you leave, as he sees the car vanish along the road, he studies the register to check who you are.

Out of these bones he has built his kingdom, his world. He knows them. He is used to them and fear of them has long since left his heart. He has sealed the nightmares behind his eyelids. Sometimes he seems to be mounting guard, to be speaking to visitors so that the skeletons on display should not reveal their own stories.

◆

He was hiding at home when the massacre took place in the church. When he heard nothing more, when the shouts, the screams, the sounds of the slaughter were silenced, he emerged. His house was surrounded by corpses.

◆

I wonder what will happen to him. Why is he there, amid these human remains, these bones? He explains, replies to questions without betraying any emotion. He touches the relics, pushes open doors, guides the visitors to the places where the remains lie in piles. He displays them as he would display anything else, as if he were in a museum. He talks, knowing that our imagination will never be able to get anywhere close to the reality. Deep down, he does not understand why we are coming to stir up Evil. Perhaps in the end all this will turn against him as he guards the evidence of our inhumanity. He cannot understand what we have come here to seek, what is concealed in our hearts. What hidden motive drives us to gaze wide-eyed at death distorted by hatred?

He was asked to be a guide because he speaks French and because he was close by during the massacre. A Hutu, and a former soldier in the national army, he had been retired for several years.

Here too, Belgian priests administered the parish: four Flemings and a Walloon. They left just before the massacre.

On the walls of the church, dried blood. The red brick is stained with purplish drips. Someone cries: 'You shouldn't have cleaned the blood off, you can hardly see anything any more!'

Holes pierce the roof. You can see the sky through the perforated sheets of iron. A solitary Virgin Mary is still standing among the debris and the overturned benches. The atmosphere is cool, as the high ceiling allows some air to circulate. People speak in whispers. A rainbow light dances from a stained-glass

15

window whose upper portion is still intact. Christ blessing his people. Jesus between two apostles. The altar is decorated with a fresco. Jesus's last supper with his disciples.

The survivors have built underground vaults where the skeletons and the remains have been piled on a number of shelves.

Forty-eight vaults here, sixty-four vaults over there.

Everything is topsy-turvy. No names. No inscriptions. Outside, the sun is beating down. Inside, there is darkness. There is no electricity. Skulls on shelves, spiders' webs and dust, and yet more dust. Everywhere, the cold odour of frozen time.

◆

From April 1994 to 1997, the bones remained as they were found. In 1997 the construction of the memorial was begun.

But the stench of death has become unbearable. Particles from the massacre are floating in the air. The dead point an accusing finger at the living who are still making use of them. The dead want to return to the earth. They rise up in protest. They want to melt into the earth.

TONIA LOCATELLI

Died 09.03.1992. RIP. (Rest in Peace.)

◆

She was an Italian nurse. Back in 1992, when the first massacres of the Tutsis began, she protested to the authorities. Faced with indifference, she launched accusations on a foreign radio station: 'We must save these people, we must protect them. It is the government itself which is doing this!'

Two days later, she was murdered by soldiers on the doorstep of her home.

They were killing in the surrounding villages, burning the dwellings. Those who resisted were disarmed and wiped out.

Not far from her grave, on an empty plot of land, a few children are playing soccer. Some baby goats bolt as we approach.

A woman of slender build moves along the road. She is tall, she must be a Tutsi. She looks at our vehicle which is raising clouds of red earth.

You cannot safely rely on physical appearance alone. Not all the Tutsis are tall. Not all the Hutus are stocky in build. Because of all the inter-ethnic marriages and the various instances of interbreeding, those chasing the Tutsis would ask first of all to see identity cards as a means of selecting their future victims.

And then, how many bones of moderate Hutus, those men and women who rejected genocide, are mingled with those of the others?

My stomach is knotted up with hunger. I haven't eaten since this morning, but I can swallow nothing. I do not want to put anything into my stomach.

◆

If we are absolutely nothing, why take the trouble to write?

ON THE ROAD TO BUTARE

Early in the morning on the winding road to Butare, in the distance the hills are making love to the sky. And their silent groans create those floating clouds you see.

17

The dusty air settles on the houses with earth-coloured walls and roofs of corrugated iron or nicely laid tiles.

I try to decipher the expressions of people we pass. Everything seems so peaceful. The hills are so green, so fertile. Terraced crops descend like giant staircases. Bicycles surge round corners, whiz down slopes, labour up the inclines, laden with all that makes up everyday life.

A child, standing on a tree branch, is watching his herd of long-horn cattle. Dotted here and there are eucalyptus trees, pines, banana trees, acacias and hibiscus bushes.

A boy is sitting at the roadside. He is almost close enough to be touched by the cars as they slalom by between the strips of tar. Sometimes, clumps of light and dark green bamboo can be seen.

Everywhere, construction is in progress.

Prisoners in their sugar-pink uniform, shorts and shirt, pass by in crocodile formation like schoolchildren.

NYANZA, THE ROYAL CITY

The same faith in a supreme being, Imana.

A single king, the mwami, half-man, half-god.

The same customs. The same language, kinyarwanda.

The basic elements: God, the king, woman, cattle.

To these must be added: Nature, man as warrior, and the all-powerful queen mother.

Of all this, almost nothing remains. Royalty has been abolished and a republic proclaimed. All vestiges of nobility have been wiped out during the successive confrontations between the 'feudal' Tutsis and the Hutu 'masses'. The wide streets of beaten earth seem to lead nowhere.

The royal drums were venerated like gods. 'The drum is

18

greater than the cry,' says the proverb. They had a 'heart', a sacred object hidden inside, whose origin was known only to the king and the priest. They were decorated with trophies of war: the genitals of enemies, the head of a defeated chief or king. The ritual objects were sprinkled with the blood of the bull-calves used for divination.

There are three breeds of cow: the most common are the short-horns; in between are the cows with medium-length horns; the noble cows have long horns the shape of a semi-circle or a lyre.

Cattle thieves were crucified.

◆

The seeds of violence have always existed, buried in the ancestral land. With the seasons they germinated and propagated, poison-grass invading the countryside.

Warrior kingdoms. Heroic violence. Courage was measured by the number of enemies killed in battle. Defeating a man, so as to strip him of his power, to seize his life force.

Who can say what makes up the memory of a whole nation? What images carpet its unconscious mind? Who can know what slaughter, hidden behind the centuries gone by, is even now sculpting the future of a nation?

CROSSING GITARAMA

In the distance, the outline of volcanoes dominates the hills. Armed soldiers are marching along the verges of the path.

We pass a line of peasant farmers going to the fields. One of them is carrying an axe.

The sun is high in the sky. The afternoon is warm and sticky.

Shapes are emerging on the horizon, standing out against the clouds. A small girl is following an old man who has his arms crossed behind his back. Women scatter suddenly as they hear the sound of the car.

Sunset on the hills.

In the distance, smoke from a bush fire snakes slowly towards the sky. A herd of cattle is drinking. The sun is a red ball behind us. The road stretches, lengthens. Night will soon be falling.

At the entrance to the town, some street kids are passing a cigarette from hand to hand.

The car headlights melt into the dusk.

My hair is powdery, heavy with dust. My skin is sticky.

VISIT TO BYUMBA

The Kubwimana family

Thérèse is always ready to laugh. Her dimples give her both a child-like air and a very motherly appearance. During the genocide, when they fled to Zaïre, she was separated from part of her family: her husband and her two boys. But a few months after the end of the war, she finally received a letter from Congo-Brazzaville telling her that the two boys were at school there and that her husband had got a job. They do not intend to come back. Before, the father was a member of the ruling party, pro-Hutu.

Thérèse lives with her three youngest children in a little house on a hill, not far from the military barracks. She is lucky, she has been able to get her old home back.

Thérèse says: 'The Rwandan people are a nation of liars. They never tell the truth to anyone.' And she bursts out laughing. She repeats this phrase several times in the course of the day.

Constance, her sister, is also very cheerful. Yet she lost almost everything in the war. She came home with her family two years ago. When they returned, their house was occupied by a soldier. After lengthy negotiations, and the intervention of the local authorities, he agreed to leave. But there was nothing left in the house. Everything had been taken.

Jean-Baptiste, her husband, was thrown into jail on their arrival, accused of having taken part in the genocide. Constance would go to see him every Friday.

For lack of proof, he was released. At the end of every month, he must go to the military centre until he is given his final release. He has no job. It is too soon. He used to be a headmaster. Now no one will give him work. Constance has a job as a teacher in a private school. They lost their eldest daughter during the war.

Their son, Isaac, was eighteen when war broke out. He got to Zaïre on foot, walking among the volcanoes. He was separated from his family, his sister, and then stayed in a refugee camp in Goma.

It was thanks to Operation Turquoise that he managed to escape. The safe humanitarian zone guarded by the French troops had in effect created a corridor through the country, thus blocking the advance of the rebel army and allowing thousands of Hutus to flee. He followed the human tide. People say that this was when those ruling the country fled with all their assets. In the huge refugee camps terrified ordinary people mingled with Hutu soldiers and perpetrators of genocide who controlled everything, imposing their own rule of law.

Isaac says little. His mind is elsewhere. He cannot bear to hear the war spoken of any longer. He has abandoned his studies and found a little job in a hospital. His parents want him to go back to school. But school no longer holds any interest for him, the future for him is too distant, too uncertain.

During the war, the militia were taking young people by force and making them fight and kill: 'If you do not kill, we will kill you. If you do not kill them, they will kill you!'

'The adults betrayed us,' Isaac thinks, 'they ruined our lives, sent us to hell, abandoned us.'

The whole country is suffering from these wounds. No one has been spared. Isaac would like to run away, but he is well aware that there is nowhere he can go.

Thérèse says I look like a Rwandan. Perhaps because of my skin colour, my hair. Later, she adds that I have black gums, a sign of beauty in the Tutsi culture.

One of the reasons for the persecution of the Tutsis comes from the theories suggested by European historians, Belgian in particular, who, towards the end of the nineteenth century, attributed to them foreign origins. According to those historians, the 'watussi' shepherds, whom they characterised as tall and slender, in contrast to the smaller Hutu farmers, were not originally natives of central Africa. Some thought they could have come from as far off as Tibet or Egypt. But the link with Ethiopia remains the most common claim. It would even seem that the Tutsis themselves have confirmed this, for their traditional costume is very similar to that worn by the Ethiopians.

There is no historical proof to verify this theory. But this claim, initially made as a form of flattery, has had terrible consequences. During the genocide, thousands of Tutsis were thrown into the waters of the Kagera river so that 'they can return to Ethiopia'.

And always, alcohol. Firstly, bottles of industrial beer are served, then beer made from the local bananas. It is drunk with a wooden straw from a calabash gourd passed from hand to hand. Then comes the distilled alcohol, whose sale is officially banned. They drink it neat, in a glass or straight from the bottle. They mix it with beer. The glasses are filled up before they are

22

empty. The bottle must be finished and another broached. It is by the number of empty bottles that you can tell how good the party was.

The voices are getting louder. People are arriving, leaving. Time passes. Introductions, more introductions: this is the Old Lady, this is an aunt, a cousin, a nephew, a brother-in-law.

A small girl climbs on to Constance's lap. She is an orphan. The family has adopted her. She was the daughter of a friend.

Thérèse shows us the photo album she has put back together. You see her two elder sons and her husband. Then the whole family as they posed for the camera. A very ordinary family in a little provincial house tucked away in the hills.

We exchange addresses.

THE LAWYER FROM KIGALI

He comes from another African country. He has already renewed his contract a number of times. He says that no one will ever really be able to understand what has happened here. Trying too hard to rationalise, you get lost in false truths. He is not involved in politics. He has his own opinion, of course, but that has nothing to do with the need for his presence here.

How can we ensure that this never happens again? 'What is needed are strong institutions, justice and national reconciliation.'

He repeats: 'Justice is what is needed. A credible justice. If people do not recognise themselves in this justice, there will be no national reconciliation.'

He believes in the death penalty. He concedes that there may be arguments against it but he thinks that it needs to exist to deal with crimes of genocide. In his opinion, the international tribunal based in Tanzania, Arusha, has a lot of resources and errs on the side of being overly humanitarian. You feel that what he would like to say is: 'They have all the time in the world and can afford to have lofty sentiments about their work. Meanwhile, however, the Rwandan prisoners are rotting in the cells of run-down and overcrowded prisons. One hundred and thirty thousand prisoners! Even the United States does not have so many. If you calculate that a thousand prisoners, maximum, can be tried in a year, how many years are we looking at?'

He does not choose whom he will defend. Sometimes they are victims, other times they are accused of having perpetrated the genocide.

There are four categories of responsibility:

- Men and women in positions of authority, that is to say those who ordered or encouraged the massacres by manipulating the people. Among these are priests, teachers, intellectuals, politicians, mayors, etc. All those who raped or killed on their own initiative;
- those who obeyed orders, who killed under duress;
- those who perhaps did not kill but who wounded or mutilated;
- those who committed economic crimes like pillage, destruction, theft and dispossession.

There are reduced sentences depending on the type of confession: spontaneous or after detention.

Before he goes, the lawyer ends: 'In the final analysis, what needs to be done is to bring some order to the chaos. I am optimistic that the Rwandans will get themselves out of this. It cannot be otherwise. If not, why am I here?'

◆

Left alone, I recall an article concerning an execution which I had read about when I was still living in Kenya.

It took about five minutes to execute the condemned prisoners, tied to stakes by their arms and legs, each one wearing a target on his chest to make it easier for the policemen to take aim.

People had come on foot and by bicycle, bringing their children to the execution site in the Nyamata stadium, not far from one of the biggest sites of the genocide.

The faces of the prisoners were hidden by black hoods. As for the policemen, they could not be identified because of the visors they were wearing.

At 11.02, that morning of 24 April 1998, the execution squad opened fire and continued to fire for four or five minutes. The crowd applauded but the atmosphere was grim.

Some bodies were still moving when a white-coated doctor came to take their pulse. A police officer with a pistol came to finish off the condemned prisoners. Then the soldiers took down the bodies, bundled them into grey blankets and took them away.

In various districts, on the same day, seventeen other prisoners had been executed.

THE MAN WHOSE LIFE WAS TURNED UPSIDE-DOWN

He has been living in Africa for a long time now. He says he was twenty-two when he left Normandy. He says that it was in Africa that he was born. Truly born. Before, he didn't exist. He couldn't feel anything. He adds: 'Western civilisation doesn't interest me. It is suffocating in its own comfort. It is sanitised, refrigerated, sated. And yet, it seeks to homogenise all nations. It was the encounter with Africa, this other world, that turned me upside-down, that gave me birth. What we have to understand is the absolute necessity of difference. The necessity of difference.'

He falls silent. He seems embarrassed. He seems to be already regretting having emerged from his thoughts. But he continues in the same tone, as if he were talking to himself: 'I know the truth of this, I am a witness to it: France ruined everything. She did not keep her promises, she betrayed this country.'

He says that he tried to tell people, to warn against skidding off the path, but no one listened to him. No one wanted to hear what he had to say.

◆

He is a man living on his dreams, on the past of this first encounter – of this revelation, this impossible love for a land which is now rejecting him. He feels torn, pulled apart by opposing forces which won't let him just be a human being.

He can no longer shake off his pessimism, or the despair taking root in his heart.

He looks lost, disorientated like a bad sailor on a boat pitching on the waves. He is seasick, and you can hear it in his voice that lacks conviction and you can see it in his face with its lines, etched too deep, too soon. You can even see it in the way he pushes back locks of hair, in an effort to tidy it, of course, but also to run his hand over his forehead in a kind of gesture of supplication.

THE WRITER

'Genocide is Evil incarnate. Its reality exceeds any fiction. How can one write without mentioning the genocide that took place?

Emotion can help us to understand what the genocide actually was. Silence is the worst thing of all. We must destroy indifference. We must understand the real meaning of the genocide, the accumulation of violence over the years.

'Is Africa's orality a handicap to the collective memory? We must write to give information some permanence. The writer pushes people to listen to his voice, in an attempt to exorcise the buried memories. He can put balm on the wound, speak of everything that may bring a little hope.

'The seed is buried in the earth. It dies so that it may be reborn.

'Dogs fed on the bodies. They were rabid. Birds fed on the eyes of the corpses.

'The fruits of peace must be gathered from the tree of suffering.

'Reconciliation?

'We must acknowledge the existence of Evil. We must exorcise it through justice, through an attempt at a true justice.

'As long as this attempt is not made, fear will remain. It is there. It has not gone away. All crime that goes unpunished will engender other crimes. The Hutus are afraid of the Tutsis because they are in power. The Tutsis are afraid of the Hutus because they can seize that power. Fear has remained in these hills.'

CONSOLATE'S STORY

Consolate has a face of astonishing sweetness. Her skin gives off reflections of copper and ivory and her graceful body sways to the rhythm of her steps.

The rain suits her as it falls in the garden and waters the flowers, dissolves time.

27

Her eyes are velvety and her smile has the taste of mango.

Sometimes, if she turns sharply, her silhouette describes a powerful arabesque. And then there is the curve of her buttocks that evokes an earthily scented love.

Consolate speaks in a hushed tone, but her words come out of her mouth with a clarity that makes you shiver. Her manner is not assertive, nor is her speech emphatic.

Her father is dead, her mother is in prison, as is her brother. Her two sisters are in the city somewhere. For her, the country is an interminable exile. She is here, but she left long ago, after the beginning of the war and the genocide. She does not recognise the land which has betrayed her and which continues to reject her, for she can find nothing to hang on to any more. Yet she has resumed her everyday activities, making those daily gestures of a life which is beginning again but which no longer has any savour. You feel that she is alone and that she will remain alone for a long, long time.

She is going to visit her mother in prison. She takes her clothes, soap, a little food. The old woman is among the crowd of other prisoners. She cannot get close to her, touch her. They speak at a distance. The distance separating them is too great. She raises her voice to make herself heard, tries to make her emotion felt above the general din, the despair. But the words vanish into the tide of jostling bodies.

She no longer recognises her mother on the other side of the invisible barrier, this broken, damaged woman who looks like nothing. She thinks that she won't come back to see her any more, because it causes both of them too much pain. In this place, mother and daughter no longer exist.

No date for the trial, no limit to her imprisonment. All her efforts to get her out have failed. The lumbering machinery has been set in motion. So Consolate tells herself that she has already lost her mother, that it is just a question of weeks, of days. The old woman has got too thin, has become too frail on her withered legs. She looks as though she is wearing a mask of pain on which wrinkles are digging long furrows. She yearns to find in her mother's eyes reflections of the past, but they are veiled by a shadow, a screen through which nothing can pass.

So, Consolate has mourned the future. The future no longer exists for her. Her days are nothing but a long anguished wait, a desire to leave for another place. The world stretches beyond the other side of those hills, far from death, far from this prison, from her captive memory, fixed, frozen in time.

Consolate goes towards the cat which has just had her first litter of kittens. The kittens are sucking greedily and the animal is purring, her eyes closed. Consolate is amazed, but from the way she cocks her head to one side, you realise that the mystery of life touches her profoundly. She cannot tear her gaze from this animal happiness, this intermingling of tiny furry bodies burying themselves in the warm fur of the blissful mother cat.

THE PROJECT MANAGER

When the war broke out, the Agricultural Project collapsed. Some of the employees are dead, others are in exile, and then there are the many of whom all trace has been lost.

After all these years, he has come back to Rwanda to find those he had left here when the genocide was going on: colleagues, drivers, trainees, secretaries, accountants. To find some trace of them, get in touch with the families of those who have died.

He has come back to pay them their wages, the money that they were never able to get hold of when the Project closed its doors, amid widespread chaos and fear.

He knows that, to some extent, he abandoned them when he boarded that plane which was evacuating foreigners, while his

Rwandan colleagues were begging him to take them with him, or at least to take their children, their wives.

Die with them? In the name of what? Of a war that was not his war? Leave. While there was still time. There had just been an earthquake and he could not recognise anything any more. There was nothing left but fear, physical fear, uncontrollable fear, of being caught in this terrifying violence that would certainly turn against them, the foreigners.

Everyone is trying in his own way to correct his mistakes, to lessen his guilt. If the Project resumes one day, he thinks that the dead will be appeased. To remember what they had done together before the genocide. To remember, so as to rebuild. He wants everything to return to order, he wants everything to be just as it was before. When the Project resumes, he will finally be at peace.

He wants to convince himself that it is possible to turn back the hands of time. He wants to free his spirit from the enormous burden of his flight. He wants absolution. He wants reconciliation. He wants forgiveness. So he is travelling the country from end to end, looking for people and finding a few.

When he returns, he will make a report to head office and he will make a case for the resumption of the Project. 'When the Project resumes,' he says, 'I can die happy.'

THE MAN WITH THE MASKS

When I arrived at his home, there were two people in the lounge. They told me he was in his study. I decided to wait for him. As soon as I sat down, I noticed opposite me a beautiful wooden statuette peeping out of a bag. Next to the two visitors, there were some more huge packages apparently containing other pieces of varying size. I realised that these were African art dealers. With all the conflicts in the region, and especially in the Democratic Republic of Congo, many antique objects can be found for sale in Kigali. The large expatriate community employed by a multitude of international organisations has created an insatiable demand.

The two men chatted to each other and looked at me with curiosity. They asked if I wanted to buy something. I declined their offer.

I got up to admire the masks hanging on the lounge walls. He came in as I did so. After a brief conversation with the dealers, he asked me: 'Are you interested in all this? Come and see.'

I followed him into a kind of vestibule giving on to a long corridor. There were masks everywhere: round masks, square masks, serene masks, frightening masks, with huge teeth, with closed mouth, with bulbous eyes, with eyes shut. Laughing masks, sacred masks, struck with astonishment. Terror masks, masks of the banned, masks of violence.

At the end of the corridor, he opened the door to his bedroom. Sacred masks trained their powerful gaze in the direction of his bed.

He knew them all, had tamed them all one at a time. When sleep was approaching, he would lie there, in the hubbub of their silence. Lying on his bed, he was nothing more than a body over which the masks mounted guard and whom they surrounded with their breath.

◆

During the day, he used to spend his time with prisoners. He would work with them in their closed world, trying to bring about some reforms and finding ways of improving their lives, even if this privilege was given only to a tiny minority, these projects being at an experimental stage.

On behalf of these men who had abandoned themselves to the orgy of slaughter, and who had become enveloped in absolute Evil, he was making gestures that might give them back a little bit of humanity.

Close your eyes? Close them to what?

Night. Walk to the bed, a poor resting place of rumpled sheets covered by a thin blanket. Immense solitude, so deep that sleep becomes a desire to fall into the abyss, to abandon oneself completely.

Arrows pierce his flesh here and there and cause him pain. Evil in its pure state, in its most extreme form, haunts his dreams. To sleep. Behind what eyelids? To dream. What nightmares?

THE JOURNALIST

In the initial days of the genocide, the members of the Hutu interim government launched a campaign of disinformation. No one realised this at the time because they appealed for international humanitarian aid, and demanded an immediate ceasefire. In this way, they succeeded in convincing the greater part of public opinion that the massacres were the result of an explosion of tribal violence as unforeseeable as it was uncontrollable.

Many of us fell into the trap. Their manners were so courteous, their language so polished and their clothes so elegant that we could not believe that they were determined to exterminate the Tutsis as well as those they considered opponents. It passed all understanding.

And then, on 7 April, all the attention was focused on the assassination of the Prime Minister, Agathe Uwilingiyimana, and of the ten Belgian soldiers responsible for her protection. The evacuation of foreign nationals, and the withdrawal of the MIN-UAR – the peace-keeping force of the United Nations – that resulted from this event became a matter of international priority.

Few journalists visited the rural areas, as they were difficult to reach, and dangerous. At the end of the war, most of the great mass graves were found in these areas.

While the genocide was going on, in South Africa Nelson Mandela was being elected to the highest office. The world preferred to turn its gaze on him to celebrate this historic moment, which marked the real end of apartheid.

The world powers knew that massacres were being carried out in Rwanda, but they were slow to react and to admit that what was going on was genocide.

A military intervention force of modest proportions could have stopped the extremists and quickly put an end to their plans. Instead, the United Nations balked at playing their part. In the end, it was France who became involved on the ground. But what role did France play? Through Operation Turquoise, the French soldiers saved lives, that is certainly true, but they also made it possible for a large number of murderers to escape using the safe humanitarian zone as a protected passage.

Consequently, it can be said that France and Belgium continued until the very end to support a genocidal regime because, as far as they were concerned, only the Hutu ethnic majority could guarantee democracy in Rwanda. But the massacres were without a shadow of doubt the result of the political manoeuvrings of the elite, who, in order to retain power, created a climate of hatred and division by urging the ethnic majority against the minority.

◆

We must all bear the responsibility for this humanitarian failure.

And still today, the conflicts continue. Sporadic but regular incursions on the part of the Hutu rebels. Attacks on and counter-attacks by the government in power.

What does the future hold? Who can swear that this won't begin all over again if hearts are filled with hatred once more? We have to dismantle the cycle of violence. We must continue to condemn every form of massacre. Every day, death weaves its fatal web.

MIGINA SUBURB, NEAR THE AMAHORO STADIUM IN KIGALI

Nelly

The tiny house has been turned into a little café-bar. The walls are painted a loud blue. An artist has drawn a fat man holding a woman by the waist in front of bottles of beer. Behind, a huge yellow condom seems to be watching over them.

Nelly is sitting in the shade of the terrace. She is wearing a hat that conceals half her face, and a long floral dress. Her body is too slender, almost skinny.

As soon as she sees us, she gets up and calls to us. She is speaking incoherently, she is gesticulating. On her face, you see large patches like a skin disease. She has smeared it with a whitish cream which gives her a pale complexion. She knows that that is all we see. She can read it in our eyes.

We sit down and start drinking the beers and Fantas she has served us. But she does not stay with us. She watches us from a distance, in silence.

Suddenly, she cries: 'Come and see my family!' and she motions us to come inside the house.

In a small room, there is a big bed with a boy of about six, asleep, his body huddled into the mattress. It is suffocatingly hot. He is sweating profusely. Hardly any light struggles through the two narrow windows.

At the foot of the bed, a girl is washing a child in a large white basin. He is crying and wriggling. His distended belly button is the mark of too short a stay in the maternity ward. The girl is beautiful. She makes very slow gestures to calm the small child. Nelly declares: 'This is my daughter. I am a grand-mother!' She goes up to the sleeping boy and murmurs: 'This one is my darling. He is a gift from God.' Roughly she seizes his arm and shakes him hard. The child opens his eyes and makes feeble protest for a few seconds. Then he goes back to sleep lying on his back. Nelly laughs uproariously and goes to the baby, whom her daughter is now smearing with Vaseline. She slaps his bottom a few times saying: 'I don't want this one. He was born of the war. What are we to do with him?' As she says this, she is preparing to hit him. Her daughter says something without raising her head. Nelly stops short, seizes the child and plants a smacking kiss on his mouth.

Nelly shows us her little kitchen garden in the yard: 'Look at that, it isn't much. But we have to make some kind of effort. There are snakes in there. I don't care because, me, Nelly, I'm not afraid of snakes. I catch them in one hand and then I hold them like this to strangle them!' She clenches her fist and raises her right hand to her face. We feel as if the snake is contorting before our very eyes.

She shrieks: 'Remember Nelly. Don't forget me. Times are very, very hard.' She begins to cry. Her voice breaks.

I go up to her and give her a banknote: 'Here's a little present for you.' She looks surprised and exclaims: 'That's a lot!' Then she grabs my arm and pulls me hard towards her to kiss me on both cheeks. I manage not to put my hands immediately to my face. She goes on thanking me but I don't hear her any more. I just want to get some water onto my face. I am thinking: 'That's what life is all about, we can't get close to people without them getting into our lives whether we like it or not.'

On the threshold, she says again: 'Remember Nelly. When I die, you must come to my funeral!'

I know very well why she says this. Her body, too thin, far too frail, is showing signs of disease.

Outside, we are blinded by the light.

IN KIGALI, THEY TELL THE FOLLOWING STORY

A widow was living alone in her house. Her husband had died during the genocide and she had seen her neighbour kill her only son. She had been raped by militiamen and abandoned on the roadside. But she had survived.

At the end of the war, she had gone back to where she lived, to her home. The neighbour had resumed his life, his activities as before.

One day, she fell seriously ill. She thought she would die. And it was this man, a nurse by profession, who came to take care of her. He looked after her for several days. Thanks to his care, she finally recovered. During his visits, they fell in love. The widow gave herself to him.

Then, the people of her neighbourhood were outraged: 'How can you live with the man who killed your own son?' And she replied: 'Where were all of you when I was ill and in pain? This man saved my life. Since the war, I have not been in good health. Who knows if I haven't got AIDS? This man is sharing my AIDS. Which of you would have done the same?'

The story does not recount if the woman is still living with the man, if they have died or if the neighbour has been denounced by others and put in jail.

We do not learn either if the man knows that the woman knows of his crime. We do not know how he came to become so involved with her. Does he know that she probably has AIDS?

Is this a true story? Was it made up to discourage inter-ethnic marriages? Was it to show how murderers are still mingling with the general population and that the do-gooders of today are perhaps yesterday's killers?

Should we condemn this woman's love? Is the man redeemed by it?

This love was born of death. Death is its beginning and its end. Death is love, the connection.

THE FIRST RETURN

Yes, I went to Rwanda but Rwanda is also here in my country. The refugees are scattered all over the world, carrying within themselves the blood and fury of the abandoned dead.

And I am afraid when, in my country, I hear people talk of who belongs there and who doesn't. Creating division. Creating foreigners. Inventing the idea of rejection. How is ethnic identity learned? Where does this fear of the Other come from, bringing violence in its wake?

One day, ordinary life disappears, giving way to chaos. Where were the seeds of hatred embedded? In the dark night of absolute blindness, what would I have done if I had been caught up in the spiralling violence of the massacre? Would I have resisted betrayal? Would I have been cowardly or brave? Would I have killed or would I have let myself be killed?

Rwanda is inside me, in you, in all of us.

Rwanda is under our skin, in our blood, in our guts. In the very depths of our slumber, in our waking hearts.

It is despair and the desire to come alive again. It is death which haunts our life. It is life which overcomes death.

◆

We must never cut off the way back.

We must understand, like a song to be hummed, that the world is still standing and that the picture we have of ourselves is absolutely real.

The Wrath of the Dead

The dead were paying regular visits to the living and when they were with them, they would asked why they had been killed.

The town streets were filled with spirits moving around, whirling in the stifling air. They jostled the living, clambered on their backs, walked alongside them, danced around them, followed them through the crowded alleyways.

The dead would have liked to speak but no one could hear them. They would have liked to say all that they had not had time to say, all the words whose utterance they had been denied, cut from their tongues, torn from their mouths.

They were in every neighbourhood. You could feel them as they scurried past people.

The spirits were hurrying home to visit everyone they had known, in the places that they had loved and which were still their own.

And even if nothing remained but houses in ruins, they needed only a stone to rediscover the days gone by.

They floated among the living who went on leading their daily lives, and whose memory was starting to fade. Wounds remained embedded in their flesh, but those wounds were slowly closing over their nightmares.

◆

The wrath of the dead faced with oblivion, with broken promises, was only to be expected. For life was already pulling at the

41

living from all sides and they no longer knew where to turn. Already they were being sucked in by the demands of daily life and its endless routine details were threatening their revolt. They were losing the desire to rebel and to reject any resemblance to an accursed past. They were astonished to rediscover the pleasure of going about their daily lives.

◆

And when they were angry, the dead gathered on empty lots among the debris, in places which had drunk of their blood and suffering and, once again, they would release the last mortal cries of their fleshly envelope. The wind carried away their rage and pierced the eardrums of the survivors. Consciences were darkened by anguish, making the days and nights unbearable.

◆

Some of the dead were so enraged that they refused to go when the time came to quit the earth. There was one in particular whose head had been cut off and who was angry with everyone. His ally was a torrential downpour.

◆

The rain fell furiously. An angry rain shrieking its refusal to open the gates to the other world. And it hammered the earth with great strokes in order to say: 'No!' To say that this dead man did not want to leave, that he had far too many things still to do, that he had loved life too much to leave it so.

'No!'

And the rain hammered on, stormed, rebelled, demanded that the spirit should remain where it was.

The dead man groaned: 'Why so soon? Why like this?

'What will become of my voice, my eyes?

'Who will continue what I have begun?'

He was scattering himself to the four winds. He moved from house to house, yard to yard, as the rain continued to fall ever harder and people stayed shut up in their homes. Everything had come to a halt.

The dead man argued, discussed, negotiated to be allowed to remain on earth. But no one would reply to him because they were walled up inside their own pain, deafened by their own tears, and their regrets.

The dead man knocked on doors and windows, but they did not open. He cried: 'Why are you abandoning me? Now I am a corpse and you no longer recognise me. Can you not feel my presence among you?'

◆

A soothsayer was brought from his dwelling far off in the hills.

When he arrived, the venerable man, a great initiate into the secrets of time, greeted the rain, turned to the wind and began to listen to the angered spirit. He heard the story of his murder, the humiliations and torture which he had undergone before he was beheaded.

When the spirit fell silent, the diviner offered many words of appeasement. Then he added: 'Even as I weep, I know that my pain can never reach even the outer limit of your suffering, you who have been mown down by cruelty. I come to humbly ask you and all the dead to receive me into the house of silence and mourning, in this dark night where memories open up like wounds. I stand before you all, dead in your thousands, so you may turn your burning gaze on my great nakedness. I am vulnerable before you, a wretch of humanity.

43

'Who am I to dare to cross the threshold of your pain? Who am I to disturb the course of your anger?

'I am the beggar in search of truth. I am the man lost in the abyss of our violence. I am he who asks you to agree to give the living another chance.'

At this moment, the soothsayer stopped.

He was brought a chicken with very white feathers, whose belly he slit open with a swift sure stroke. He pulled out the entrails and sat on the ground to study them and decipher the hidden signs. He looked at them for a long time with great concentration. When he thought he had found what he was looking for, he made some ritual offerings and spat into the wind words that no one could catch.

Suddenly, the rain began to calm so that only the regular murmur of its lamentation could be heard, the refrain of its despair.

And soon, the first noises of daily life could be heard: bursts of talking, shouts, objects being moved, engines thrumming, machinery working somewhere at the end of the street, music coming from a radio. The inhabitants came out of their shelters and hesitantly set out on the muddy roads. The rolling of thunder came now only from a distance. Nature seemed to be peaceful again at last.

Then the dead man knew that his rebellion must come to an end. He prepared himself for the journey which was to take him to the other side of existence. When not a single drop more rain fell from the sky, he had gone.

◆

The diviner spoke to the living as follows:

'What we must do now is bury the dead according to our rites, bury their desiccated bodies, their bones growing old in the open air, so that we keep of them nothing but their memory, heightened by respect. Memory is like a sword dipped in steel, like rain in the heart of drought. A tiara placed on the head of a tearful princess, finery over the shoulders of a mother bruised by sorrow, a garment of light to drape over a man broken by the immensity of absence and make him beautiful.

'We must bury the dead so that they may return to visit us in peace, and hide their decay and their blinding nakedness, so that they do not place a curse on us. We must give back to the images of life the right to assert themselves, so that these bones covered in dust and violence will not bear the burden of the hatred which buried them.

'We must ask them to yield up to us the secrets of life, which becomes triumphant once more, since only the living can bring the dead back to life. Without us, they no longer exist. Without them, we fall into emptiness.'

The diviner stopped for a moment to make sure that everyone had understood his words and also to gather strength.

He went on:

'It is the dead themselves who are asking us to go on living, to resume our activities, to speak again those words they can no longer say themselves.

'How could they come back if we bar their way with our despair and our tears?

'We must open the door to them, let them settle in, show them how we are living, remembering them through love, friendship and duty.

'How strange is their eternal universe! Souls, burdened by all their wounds and mutilations, are judged and received at the divine tribunal. What rites can cleanse these abandoned corpses, devoured by dogs and crows? Take their saddened souls by the hand and lead them to the road to freedom, through the dazzling light, up the fiery staircase, in the bright dawn of all creation, the dawn of the morning sun and the dew lying on its grassy bed.

'For time does not grow old. Three hundred and sixty-six days or the lightning passage of a second are all the same. The past and the future are the same distance, always bringing us back to the already completed moment.'

The diviner suddenly changed his tone and began to speak with a kind of serenity which quickly spread:

'The dead will be reborn in every fragment of life, however small, in every word, every action, however simple it may be. They will be reborn in the dust, in the dancing water, in the children who laugh and play as they clap their hands, in every seed hidden beneath the black earth.

'And the spirits will depart to wherever they desire, no longer as spirits in torment but as flashes of lightning.

'We must cast down all the evil which has been done so that the dead can sleep in peace and so that life may be relieved of the burden of our guilt.

'We shall quieten the sound of our voices which are too loud to listen to the murmurs from under the earth.

'They will tell us how to purify our passions, clean away the dust, throw away the stones that burden our lives.

'We beg the dead not to increase the misery in which the country is wallowing, not to come and torment the living, even though they may not deserve their forgiveness.

'We ask them to recognise our humanity, even though we are weak and cruel.

'We have sullied the earth, plundered the sun. We have trampled on hope.

'Nevertheless, we ask the dead not to seek revenge. Not to ill-treat us by sending a swirling horde of demons on to our heads. Not to send upon us a terrible drought which will lay waste our fields. Not to eat our entrails, not to tear out our eyes, not to engulf our future. We ask them not to let our hearts burn in the fire of our existence.

'We shall search for phrases to appease them, prayers to soften their hearts, words we need so that they do not abandon us in the middle of what we are doing, so that our lives do not become endlessly tormented.

'May their spirits rise to heaven so that they may find the kingdom that is theirs and to which we can have no access. May they remain the stars of our firmament, those we see in the dark night and which will still be shining for generations to come. May they populate our dreams with their cold splendour.

'None among us has ever returned from that kingdom of theirs to tell us how they are, whether they have at last found peace or if they are seeking shelter. No one has told us whether they are still carrying within them the memory of the wounds and mutilations of our fratricidal hatreds. No one can tell us how they will greet us when the time comes for us to go and join them. Our fear is infinite, for we fear to be banished for eternity, to be exiled in torment by their tribunal.'

Then the voice of the diviner became hard and sharp:

'Men and women, guard against a desire for vengeance and the perpetual cycle of violence and reprisals. The dead are not at peace because your hearts are still shot through with hatred. The ashes of war are still smouldering.

'The signs augur ill. We must not deceive ourselves, the present is not what it should be. Too many injustices remain rooted in the heart of our country. The young are paying for the mistakes of their elders. Hordes of adolescents, their memory white-hot, are roaming the country. Hope is rare. Very few believe in the birth of a new future.

'Will reconciliation be achieved one day?

'You live together, but look in opposite directions. You co-habit to survive, but no one is willing to take the first step.

'The signs are telling us: the nation is in mourning. Pain comes in waves. But when those waves threaten to engulf you, remember that you are the masters of your emotions.'

◆

So saying, the diviner turned on his heel and disappeared into the hills, the thousand hills of this country.

His Voice

Isaro was writing when the phone rang. She picked up the receiver and recognised the voice immediately. After all these years, here he was speaking to her at last! And the words he was speaking at the other end of the line brought back all the memories like waves breaking on the shore.

Initially it was the physical sensation of his presence that overwhelmed her. She felt as though he was standing there, in front of her, ready to touch her. She was disturbed, astonished, caught off guard. She felt herself coming back to life, invaded by an uncontrollable desire to see him again. How had his voice been able to travel across time to reach her?

When she replaced the receiver after arranging to meet in a café the following morning, she tried to make herself see reason. She simply had to protect herself if she wanted to avoid a huge disappointment. After all, even though his voice was the same, this man's face probably wouldn't be the same as Romain's. She would have to be careful if she didn't want to get hurt. Very hurt. She had already suffered a great deal like this. It had taken years to get over her husband's death. Years during which she had felt alone, thinking that any possibility of happiness had died with him. She had felt her body wither.

◆

Isaro went over to the window. Night was falling. There was nothing that she wished for now. Only the gathering darkness filled her mind. The sky was taking on a purplish hue. Everything seemed peaceful. The branches of the trees swayed softly, leaves quivering gently in the evening breeze.

Her mind wandered. She saw once more the lifeless body of Romain, motionless and cold. Nothing had prepared her for that.

◆

Isaro got up early. She took a long shower and dried herself with care and rubbed cream into her body. Then, she smoothed her hair with sweet almond oil to give it more lustre.

Choosing the right outfit proved more difficult. She wanted to feel comfortable as well as elegant. Not too elegant. Just enough for this first encounter.

After much hesitation, she chose matching trousers and top in a coloured fabric. She did not like dresses. Above all, she was anxious not to draw attention to her appearance. First, she must make sure that it was really him, that his mind was really that of Romain. She wanted to be able to see this man's true nature.

When she was ready, she realised that she was very calm, very sure of what she was doing.

◆

He had given a good description of himself. She moved straight to the table where he was seated, a little set back. He rose to greet her. His handshake was warm.

Her heart lurched a little when she saw how different he was from Romain, taller, heavier in build. But she was not discouraged. It was his spirit she was trying to recover.

While they were talking, she listened attentively to the

cadences of his voice, looking for signs that might confirm the presence of Romain. Yes, now and then, she could recognise him. But as the conversation progressed, this feeling diminished. The man's physical presence was too powerful to preserve the fragile memory of Romain.

And yet, she liked the man who was talking to her. He had a beautiful smile. His hands were huge, like those of a farm labourer or a carpenter. He wore a hat that covered his hair and gave him a deceptively casual air. He was a cautious man who weighed his words and paid attention to others. His voice had not betrayed him. He seemed sincerely happy to meet her. The conversation was easy, free. Had he, too, been looking forward to this meeting?

For her, it was important to listen carefully in an attempt to make up for lost time. There was no room for lies or games.

Isaro realised that she was asking him far too many questions, but she couldn't help herself. She wanted to find out as much as possible about him.

But something unexpected happened: a bee came buzzing around their heads. The insect flew around them and came close to their faces. As it went towards the mouth, eyes, nose, hair of one of them, the other would watch the scene without attempting to intervene for fear of angering the insect. The bee was particularly attracted to Isaro. The conversation became disjointed, its thread lost. They found it impossible to concentrate. They tried to ignore the insect, but in vain. They felt tense. Now Isaro wanted to leave.

'I think it is time for me to go,' she said, rising from her seat.

'It must be the oil in your hair,' he said in reply.

'Yes, that's what it must be, and it's the last time I use it!'

She felt ridiculous. Their meeting was going to end on a sour note. She was not leaving, she was running away, and as quickly as she could to avoid being stung. He must really think it a shame that an insect could thus change the course of their meeting.

◆

Isaro went home, disappointed. What had she been hoping for? That Romain would return as simply as that? And besides, what had she done for him to return? She had contented herself with waiting for him, counting the days. Yes, since his death, she had done nothing but count the days, the months, the years. She had surrounded herself with the things that had belonged to him.

◆

That evening, she went to bed early. That was the best thing to do.

But her sleep was restless, filled with flashing images that appeared and vanished again. The hanged body of Romain. His stiffened limbs. His swollen face. The terrible discovery. The overwhelming grief.

Isaro woke with a start, drenched in perspiration. A night of bad dreams. She drank a glass of water. 'Why had he done it?' The question spun around in her head without ever finding an answer. 'Why did he kill himself? What can be done now to clear his name of all those accusations?'

He was no longer here to defend himself. Doubt would remain forever etched in people's memories.

◆

Yet, they had done their best to resume a normal life after the war. She had been able to get back her job as a secretary, and even though her salary was very small, they had been able to

54

manage. For Romain, things were a lot more difficult. He had not been able to bear being unemployed. Even though he went knocking on doors looking for work, no one had wanted him: 'Where were you during the genocide?' How many times had he heard that question?

Then, one day the accusations had started. His name had come up in various testimonies. He was accused of having taken part with a group of militia in the murder of a whole family. What had happened at Nkuranya's house on the evening of 15 May, 1994? Who had killed his wife and three children?

Isaro didn't know. At the beginning of the war she had been separated from Romain. They had only been reunited at the end.

What had happened at Nkuranya's house? Where was Romain that evening? Why had he been named? Was his suicide proof of his guilt? How she would have liked to have had an answer to these questions.

They had never talked of what Romain had experienced during their separation. He had told her that he had taken refuge with his elder brother. Today, she bitterly regretted not having asked him more questions.

◆

She thought she saw accusations in every gaze: 'Where was your husband during the genocide? And you, where were you?' She would have liked him to have been tried, so as to be cleared of all suspicion. But this would never be possible now. He had killed himself. He had taken the truth with him.

A few days before his death, Romain had asked her: 'Do you believe that I am innocent?' She had hesitated a few seconds, nothing significant, but she had not met his gaze when she replied: 'Of course I do. I wouldn't be with you if I didn't.'

Isaro had lied to him knowing that he would realise that she had.

She would have liked to crush this doubt which obsessed her day and night. When would she feel free of it? What rite was needed for her to get back her peace of mind?

◆

She thought again about the meeting. It was ridiculous. Had she left because of a bee? He must have thought her behaviour silly, childish.

◆

Isaro remembered Romain's burial. Very few people attended, only a few family members. She had not told the priest that Romain had committed suicide.

It was after the ceremony that she had been overwhelmed by the full force of grief. Before, there had been practical details to take care of, registering his death, papers to be dealt with. She had refused to tidy his things, leaving everything just as it was. Exactly like before. He would come back one day, she was sure of it. And what would he think if everything had been removed? If none of his things had been kept?

Isaro kept telling herself that, as things have a soul, Romain would reveal himself through them. Yes, she had been expecting his return for a long time now.

◆

Isaro woke up with difficulty. She washed her face in cold water and went to gather her thoughts before the little altar raised in memory of Romain. Then she went to the phone and called the man she had met. She apologised for her hasty departure of the previous day.

Isaro once more had the impression that she was listening to Romain. But that did not matter so much any more. They agreed to meet that afternoon, in the same place.

◆

Isaro found him sitting at the same table, set back a little. He greeted her as if he had known her a long time.

'I have lost those I loved the most in the genocide,' he said. 'I will never forget them. Never. They will be with me all my life and I know that no one can ever replace them. But after all these long years, I know that I must not let time stand still. We must carry our memories of them within us and let those memories become part of our daily lives. We must not separate memory from life – we must integrate it.'

'They will return some day, I am certain of it!' cried Isaro.

'No, they will never return,' he said firmly. 'They will never be with us again.'

Then Isaro's head drooped.

'Time is watching us,' he went on. 'It is watching what we do with the death of others. If we fail, there will be no more hope. Those who have gone have left us the earth in which their bones lie buried. It is up to us to rebuild life. Our long vigil must come to an end.'

'But there are still too many unanswered questions. If the dead come back to reclaim their due, what will we have to give them?'

'The dead will not return to claim anything, for they have embarked on another existence. And we will never have all the answers to our questions. We must punish those who deserve to be punished, those who began the reign of cruelty. But the others must be freed of the burden of guilt.'

Isaro remained silent. She was realising that no one had ever spoken to her in this way. It seemed to her that this man had penetrated the secrets of her soul.

'I think that it is time you told me your name,' she murmured.

'My name is Nkuranya,' he said. 'Nkuranya.'

Anastase and Anastasie

For the first time, he had the impression of helplessness, of ignorance and incapacity. Instead of confronting death head on, he was fleeing it. Instead of descending into the bowels of the earth, he was drawing back, terrified by the infinite choices of that other life. Where had Anastasie gone?

His head was spinning. He no longer knew what was going on. The air was burning the inside of his body. Nature was withdrawing from him.

He felt crushed by the enormity of her disappearance.

He had lost Anastasie at the very moment when he had hoped to bring her back, not only as his sister, but as the woman he had loved and with whom he had so much in common. He had thought that the wounds would begin to heal, all those self-inflicted wounds from before the war, and the wounds that had come after. But the sores remained open. What was he to do now?

The sky was nothing but a black carpet on which the clouds were sliding to infinity, a drifting mass edged with light. And suddenly, a rent appeared, a shaft of blood-red light in the flesh of the sky.

Now, before his eyes, the vault of the heavens was opening up to let daylight take possession of it. A phosphorescent trail, a blazing inferno springing from the coolness. Anastase was drawing close to the moment of the sun's rebirth.

This energy, this fusion, is that where souls vanished to bring to it all the force of their energy? Is that where the sum of all desire and all disappointment gathered?

The memory of Anastasie wandered slowly along the byways of his memory. Her scent was inside him. The taste of her skin was still fresh and the sound of her voice resounded in a hundred echoes. Nostalgia remained intact.

'This mountain standing before me,' he thought, 'I have got to move it. I must stretch out my hands and catch the bird in flight. I must eat the earth in great mouthfuls, reply to the call of the wind. I must learn to live without her, on the other side of time.'

What he most feared was to open the gates of memory and feel the emptiness go to his head, becoming drunk with solitude. What was he to make of the death of Anastasie?

Anastasie would wake suddenly as dawn was breaking and be invaded by the memory of her rape. Though the sun might show its laughing face, she did not see it. She was trapped in the prison of her flesh. Her tongue felt furry, and prevented her from uttering the slightest word. Her desires had been worn away like rocks lashed by a stormy sea. She no longer recognised the inside of her body, felt a stranger to this heavy mass which was crushing her spirit. She felt exhausted even before glimpsing the beginning of the day. She would have liked to have been able to sleep longer, to seal her eyes more hermetically. To disappear into oblivion, sail gently along, let herself be carried away by the underground stream. Shut the door to the shouts and murmurs of life, to the grating sound of the revolving door of time. A steady slide. Loss of consciousness. It was so much better deep in her bed. More comforting, more peaceful. She could revisit her favourite places, re-create the special moments when, as a little girl with no cares or responsibilities, she would skip along the path down the hill. There was not a tree, not a bush, not a hiding place that she did not know.

Why did tomorrow always lead to suffering? She had felt it in her brother's face, in his despair, his clouded eyes, his already bitter mouth.

Anastasie was welded to the darkness, eyes wide open to hostile dreams, wondering if the morning light could wipe out her memory of the years emptied of all sweetness.

Daylight's only purpose was to keep her awake until she could sleep again.

Despite the passage of years, she still bore the wound in her flesh, in her hair, in her smile. She felt fragile, vulnerable. What was she to do with all these bad feelings that jostled in her head and left so little room for anything else?

What frightened her deep within herself was the way in which her thoughts were scattered, preventing her from concentrating on anything. Instinctive terrors kept coming back to haunt her. Then she would cry:

'I reject you, I spit on you, I vomit on you all. You have betrayed me. You have destroyed my future!'

◆

But Anastase plucked up courage to write to her, tell her that he was thinking of her, that he had never stopped thinking about her, and that he begged her forgiveness for having hurt her. 'Please reply, I beg you,' he said. 'Break this silence which is causing me so much pain.'

Anastasie held the letter in her trembling hands. However much she tried to read and re-read the words, she could not lessen the beating of her heart. How dared he write those lines, believing that they might still have something in common? Her throat tightened and she felt as though she had been slapped in the face.

She was frightened. Could she get herself out of this maze? Could she find herself again? 'Doesn't he understand all the harm he has done me? Doesn't he know he has destroyed me?'

◆

In the depth of her sleep came despair. Her eyes were closed and her mind was breaking free to fly over the whole universe, but she still had the physical sensation of drowning slowly. She was sinking, sinking to the point where the rhythm of her breathing was lost. Then she awoke with a start, opening her eyes on the complete and irresistible emptiness.

She knew that henceforth her body was inhabited by Evil. There was no room in her life for frivolity any more.

◆

Motionless, Anastase stood in the corridor listening to the sounds of the household. It was two o'clock in the morning. Everything seemed calm. He could just make out Anastasie's regular breathing and the more rapid breathing of her two younger brothers in the next room. He shut their door and listened again. No sound came from down below.

He tip-toed into his sister's room. He approached the bed where she lay asleep on her back. Using his torch he saw that she was wearing a white T-shirt and that she had pushed the sheet down to her waist.

Anastasie woke with a start as the naked light swept her face. She tried to cry out, but Anastase was too quick for her, putting a hand over her mouth to prevent her. With his other hand, he had placed the point of a knife against her neck. 'Shut up and don't move, or I'll hurt you! I'll cut you up. You think I haven't seen you flirting with boys? You're behaving like a prostitute!' Feeling Anastasie struggle, he increased the pressure of the knife on her skin. He heard a muffled scream.

Now his sister, terrified, wasn't moving any more.

Anastase let go a moment or two and seized a wrapper hanging near the bed. Then, using it as a large bandage, he covered her eyes and mouth. He tied the material so tight that

Anastasie thought she would suffocate. 'Don't move,' he repeated, 'or you'll be sorry!' When he spread her legs and entered her violently, she could not believe that what was happening to her was real. This must be in another life, another time. Her mind ceased to function.

Anastase left her lying there, on the soiled bed.

She lay there prostrate, terrified.

She was ashamed. She felt dirty, repulsive. She no longer existed.

How was she ever going to be able to get up? Face other people?

Her mind detached itself from her body, floated in the room and hit the ceiling.

That was her first death.

Officially, Anastasie died several years later, towards the end of April 1994. No one is really sure of the exact date of her death for, in her neighbourhood, very few people lived to tell the tale. However, all the eye-witness accounts agree. Despite her youth, Anastasie belonged to a resistance group which held off the militia for several weeks. The militia had to call for reinforcements of soldiers and police to defeat them.

All the residents had joined together to erect barricades to prevent the attackers entering the area. They had fought night and day. But the killers finally infiltrated the area. Houses, schools, churches were set on fire. The killing began. All the Tutsis and those who had tried to defend them were massacred.

Those Who Were Not There

KARL

Karl was abroad, visiting his country of origin, when the events took place. When he heard on the radio that the presidential plane had been shot down and that the Head of State was dead, he had rushed to the phone and had a long conversation with Annonciata. Yes, there was trouble in town, she had said, but for the moment their neighbourhood was calm. The children were well. However, the schools had been closed.

Karl had advised them to be very careful and not to go out if possible.

But when, the following day, and in the days to come, he realised the extent of the danger, it was already too late. The telephone lines had been cut.

Air traffic to and from Rwanda had been suspended. Karl now found himself completely cut off from his family. This was crazy. How could he get them out of the country as quickly as possible? Faced with the impossibility of contacting the Rwandan embassy, he had called the Ministry of Foreign Affairs to find out if they had some recent news of the situation in Rwanda. Nobody had been able to give him a sensible answer.

Confusion reigned. A Private Secretary kept repeating nervously that, on the ground, the evacuation of nationals from his country was being organised. What nationality was his partner? Rwandan? Impossible. And the children? Perhaps, he would see

71

what he could do. His family should make contact with the Red Cross as quickly as possible.

Now, Karl was seeing the televised images: bodies everywhere, strewn along the roads, the streets. Columns of refugees fleeing, carrying their sparse belongings on their heads. Children crying, women walking, fear in their eyes. He thought that at any moment he would recognise his children, and their mother, among the nameless crowd of refugees or among the inert bodies lying here and there.

And yet, even before his departure, there had already been a tense atmosphere in Kigali. The tone was hardening. The radio was broadcasting hate slogans. Everyone knew that something terrible was in the air, that new waves of anti-Tutsi persecution were getting ready to break as they had in the past. But genocide, no. No one had imagined anything on such a scale.

How could they have been so blind?

◆

It was in Rwanda that he had decided to rebuild his life. It was in Rwanda that his friends lived. He realised now that he should have married Annonciata, should not have put off making their relationship legal. But back then, he thought he had plenty of time. Now, he could not stop reproaching himself for not having done it. It might have given her the right to be evacuated. It might have saved her. He lost years of hope in this apocalypse. Life was certainly not doing him any favours.

◆

What torments him most today is that he let himself be persuaded that it was better not to go back to Annonciata and the children. His own parents had said to him: 'It wouldn't help to go back there. What can you do in all that chaos? You'll be killed before you can find them. Stay here until the situation stabilises. You'll be more useful to them alive than dead!' But he knew that his father and mother had never understood his attachment to this little country lost on the map of the world. They had never been happy about his relationship with Annonciata.

Karl told himself that, when he got back, nothing would be left of his past life, that he would have to start again from scratch.

He lived like a caged beast in his home town. He had nowhere to go. He could find no way to lessen his suffering and calm his distress. He could not free himself of the crushing feeling of guilt that he had not been able to protect his family, that he had in some way abandoned them to their fate at the very moment when they needed him most. He had left them alone to face the greatest peril, the most terrible suffering.

◆

At last, in July, he had heard through the Red Cross that his family had been found in a refugee camp.

As soon as flights were resumed, he flew to Kigali.

Their reunion was the most intense experience of his life.

His family was safe and sound. Nothing else mattered. The relief he felt was intoxicating, for it marked the end of his suffering.

◆

The country was in ruins, the horror still palpable. The stench of rotting flesh pervaded Kigali.

He had arrived as they were busy cleaning up the city, and

73

watched, stock-still, as soldiers of the victorious army shot at stray dogs, rabid beasts that had gorged themselves on the abandoned corpses. During those hundred days of that orgy of blood, screams and rage – bursting flesh and stench of meat exposed to the sun – the dogs had feasted on the bodies of their masters.

The country was not the same any more.

Nothing was as it had been before.

But to be able to clasp his children in his arms gave him the hope and the strength to rebuild.

◆

Daily life resumed. They had to learn to live side by side once more.

As time passed, however, Karl realised that he had lost his partner, the mother of his children, Annonciata, the woman he had known and loved. The woman who had seduced him with her energy and her high spirits was only the shadow of her former self.

◆

After their return home, she had fallen ill without anyone knowing exactly what was the cause. Retreating into herself, she wouldn't speak, took no interest in anything any more, had completely lost her appetite. She spent her days in bed, and at night she lay awake, eyes staring, motionless.

Karl tried to talk to her, bring her out of her isolation, but in vain. When he came close to her, he felt her stiffen, trying to avoid any contact. He could not touch her or even kiss her or hold her in his arms. She had withdrawn from the world.

He thought that she still needed time to recover from all that she had experienced. So he put all his efforts into the children, who, in any case, refused to be separated from him.

As a last resort, Karl took his wife to a doctor who had been recommended to him. Tests, blood tests, X-rays. They waited.

Annonciata had AIDS.

◆

One evening, as he sat at her bedside, she had gathered her last reserves of strength and confessed her suffering to him. She had been raped by militiamen several times on the side of the road. She had bargained for the lives of her children. For nights on end, the men guarding the barrier had made use of her.

◆

Today, Karl cannot manage to wipe the past from his memory, or emerge from his mourning which has lasted several years now. He wants to punish himself, to sentence himself to extended suffering.

One day, perhaps, his children may succeed in freeing him from his pain. With their immense desire to live, to see life go on, perhaps, little by little, they will be able to break the chains of his infinite grief.

SETH AND VALENTINE

He is a man of average height, smooth-skinned and handsome. He has great control over his body and his bearing is that of an aristocrat. His smile is warm and his gaze over his entourage is filled with tolerance. Perhaps he is an optimist by nature or is it simply that he stands above the hurly-burly of life?

He is very well dressed – probably designer garments. His shirt and trousers are elegantly cut. But the colour of his jacket is rather ordinary, too classical, which suggests that he may be quite conventional.

Speaking to him, it quickly becomes obvious that his is an ivory tower existence, and that he has been brought up to have a high opinion of himself.

When the massacres of 1963 took place, his paternal uncle sent him out of the country with his brothers and sisters. His father, a senior civil servant, and his mother, a pharmacist, had been assassinated, at home, in Rwanda.

His life in Burundi began at the age of four. Today his memory of Bujumbura is a very happy one, filled with a feeling of paradise regained, idyllic, and convinced that they should have been able to live like that in Kigali.

His first love will probably be his last. Valentine waited for him five years, while he was completing his studies in the States. Then she joined him. Two years later, they returned to Burundi for the wedding ceremony.

Seth tells me in great detail about the visit to the in-laws, arms laden with gifts, the symbolic sum of the dowry to be paid and the lengthy negotiations. He bursts out laughing: 'My uncle, who wasn't very familiar with Burundian customs, almost ruined the whole ceremony. When it came to handing over the dowry, he didn't understand what he was supposed to do. The Elders did their best to guide him, but as he really had no idea what was required, they were obliged to withdraw. There was a moment of uncertainty when everybody looked at each other in embarrassment. So, a representative of the in-laws got up and whispered something in my uncle's ear and finally we were able to get on with the ceremony.' He laughs again just at the thought. In fact, he is delighted by all of this. He feels that in Burundi tradition is still alive, whereas in Rwanda traditional practices have almost completely disappeared as a result of the abolition of the monarchy and the all-pervasiveness of Catholicism.

Seth speaks of his wife with admiration. He brings out a picture of his daughter. The child is smiling broadly. She looks like her father.

During his last trip to Burundi, he spent a few weeks in Rwanda. He thinks the situation is improving, that the signs are good. 'We have hit rock bottom. Now we are going to move up again.' He believes that much can be done for the country. He is preparing to return: 'In two years, if all goes well, Valentine will have her degree. She will be able to get a job there and I will set up a business.'

I look at him. Suddenly, I am concerned about him. Leave the United States for Rwanda with his whole family? The call of the country is indeed powerful. It is like the life-blood that pulses through the veins and arteries and makes the heart swell.

The Second Journey

SABENA FLIGHT 565

I am sitting next to a woman who is part of the Dian Fossey Foundation. We are talking about the gorillas. They are Rwanda's principal tourist attraction.

In the far north of this tiny country, the last 'silverbacks' are living on the heights of the chain of volcanoes. The mountains stretch across Rwanda, the Democratic Republic of Congo and Uganda. On the Rwandan side, the Volcano National Park has been given over to their use. Dian Fossey had made of it a kingdom.

Strange vegetation plunged into a thick fog, territory lost in eternal mists, it is here that the mountain gorillas have chosen to make their home. In this silent space, outside of time and far from humans, dense bamboo forests, gigantic plants, prehistoric flora and long-haired trees stand guard over these majestic animals. And the mossy carpets, replete with dampness and stagnant water, stretch as far as the banks of the lakes huddled inside craters.

During the whole period of the genocide and war, the great primates were not harmed. They took refuge in the mountain peaks. But people say that in any case none of the fighters would have attempted to harm them. Is it the mystery of their imposing presence that has made them into totem-animals? Or is it simply because they are symbolic of a beauty that passes our understanding?

And yet, for a long time, their immense size was a reason for men to hunt them. Coming from Europe with their sophisticated weapons, or simply from the surrounding villages, the hunters wanted to get themselves a trophy and in that way to conquer the fear that they felt of these creatures from another world. Men sought to proclaim themselves, once again, the uncontested lords of creation.

Dian Fossey is dead, probably murdered by poachers. In the end she had loved animals more than the human race.

Before the gaze of dumbfounded villagers, foreigners would arrive with their enormous cameras and their plans for some expensive project and disappear into the mountains, without looking back. This was not good.

Yes, it is true that once upon a time the villagers used to hunt the gorillas, but what did they know then of the terrifying creatures with their frighteningly human appearance? It took the establishment of the research station for them to understand that these creatures were Rwanda's most precious possession. More precious than themselves? The competition was on.

'Who killed the tourists travelling on the Ugandan side of the chain of volcanoes?'

They were looking for the mountain gorillas, wanted to get close to them, watch them in all the splendour of their freedom. According to the most common version of events, they were the victims of the Interahamwe who, still unable to accept defeat, are infiltrating the country and launching attacks along the borders which cross the chain of volcanoes.

La Nouvelle Revue, a fortnightly publication in Kigali, writes: 'At dawn on 1 March, about one hundred and fifty men armed with machetes, spears and AK 47 rifles, identified as Rwandan Hutu rebels – Interahamwe, responsible for the Rwandan genocide of 1994 – attacked three camps in the impenetrable Bwindi forest in the South-west of Uganda. They tried to kidnap about thirty foreigners, but managed in the end to take only fourteen, apparently after separating the Anglo-Saxons from the French-speakers, releasing the latter.'

I ask my travelling companion if she is not frightened. She gives me another version of events. The tourists were not supposed to die. No one really wanted to harm them. It was just that the scales of chance were tipped by an unfortunate circumstance. They found themselves in the wrong place at the wrong time. As far as the authorities are concerned everything is back to normal. The chain of volcanoes is peaceful once more.

Research activity is being resumed. The National Park has reopened its doors to the public. The country needs money, foreign exchange. Jobs, camps, hotels, improvements to the environment are all scheduled. Fossey has been replaced by a young woman scientist just as committed as she was. A satellite surveillance system will track the movements of the primates with its artificial eye. It seems as though the University of Butare will also benefit from the equipment.

My neighbour is from the United States. This is not her first trip to Rwanda, it's her sixth. Press conferences, negotiations, discussions, if you want to see the silverbacks, there are humans to be dealt with first.

Do the great apes know what happened at the foot of the mountains? Were they aware of the carnage, did they sense death as it spread across the territory of humans?

KIGALI

Kimihurura, Cadillac country

The sound of birdsong enters my room. Behind the curtains, there is daylight. Everything seems peaceful. The house is silent. The room is, as yet, bathed only in half-light. My rumpled bed still has the scent of night. In the nearby rooms, my friends are sleeping.

The birds are chattering to each other, replying. In the distance can be heard the sound of the city. There are sounds from the highway: cars, motorbikes. There are dogs barking, voices shattering the dawn.

Gradually, my body comes to life again, my mind gets ready to face the day.

NO PERSON KILLED ANOTHER PERSON SINGLE-HANDED

'By mobilising fear and hatred against the Tutsis, the organisers hoped to forge a kind of solidarity among the Hutus. But beyond that, they intended to build a collective responsibility for the genocide. People were encouraged to involve themselves in group killing, like soldiers in a firing squad who all receive the order to fire at the same instant, so that no individual can be held separately accountable or solely responsible for the execution. "No person killed another person single-handed," declared one of those who participated.'

I shut the book and put it down on the table. I am breathing deeply. I cannot help reading the title again: *Aucun Témoin ne*

Doit Survivre. Le Génocide au Rwanda (Let No Witness Survive. The Genocide in Rwanda). *

Yes, to remember. To bear witness. That is what remains for us in our attempt to combat the past and restore our humanity.

KICUKIRU DISTRICT

Kagarama Sector

Everything is covered in dust. The leaves on the trees have turned to russet, the sky is heavy and dense. The weather is so dry that your skin is cracking. The sun's rays slant down, on to the weary grass, exhausted by the scorching wind.

In this area, numerous massacres took place. The site of Nyansa is a short distance away. Almost twenty thousand dead. The authorities had told most of the people to gather in the primary school and nearby. Some came from a distance, had fled their own area.

The track leading to the Youth Centre is completely broken up, damaged by potholes. It makes driving difficult.

At the entrance to the courtyard, tents have been erected. That is where children and adolescents sleep on the wooden beds they have made themselves. In one of the rooms of the main building, a group is having an art lesson. It is dark. They are absorbed in their work. The teacher raises his head to greet us. In the other room, youths are busy spreading glue over bits of paper which will later be used to make cardboard furniture. We go into the kitchen. A large pot of vegetables is cooking over the fire. Outside, in the courtyard, some small girls are

* Human Rights Watch, International Federation of the Leagues of Human Rights, *Aucun Témoin ne Doit Survivre. Le Génocide au Rwanda*, Karthala, Paris, 1999, p. 892.

getting water from black plastic tanks. A youth is repairing a coal stove with energetic blows from a hammer. The others watch him. Further off, some rabbits in their cages.

Items of cardboard furniture are lined up against the wall. Tiny chairs, shelves, tables, green, blue and yellow easy chairs. The paint is drying in the sun. They need to get orders to make a bit of money.

◆

When they first come to the Centre, the children say that they are orphans. But sometimes, after a few months, some of them begin to talk. They say where they have come from and why they left, one day, to live a wandering life. If you push them to talk, to speak of their former life, they retreat further into lies, lies that shield them against the cruelty of adults. They will tell you what you want to hear.

It is only at night, when darkness has fallen, that occasionally you will hear a few snatches of the truth. The fragments of their stories overlap with each other, and finally, a picture emerges.

Rebellious kids, rejected by society. The whole town belongs to them. Despite their faces of miniature men and women, their childhood – attempting to blossom at the edge of their smile – is still apparent. How can a gaze be so beautiful when it has seen so much misery? How can the tone of a voice still be so clear when it has been flayed by so many screams, soaked by so many tears?

Orphaned by war, AIDS, or family dislocation, when they were not roaming the streets, they spent their days at Kigali's rubbish dump. A treasure hunt: rummaging in the garbage for the leftovers of the capital.

One day, they heard of the Youth Centre and decided to go there. But they know that many of their friends have stayed at the dump. So, every now and then, they go off to visit them, along with the Centre's organisers. What do they say to each other when they meet again?

◆

Columns of smoke are rising from the ground – rubbish being burnt – a smell of rotting, of acid air which gets into your eyes, your nose, your mouth. Your lungs are swollen with dust. Your feet poke about among the rubbish. The corpse of a dog, paws in the air, is slowly swelling in the sun. Its puffy eyes stare at the leaden sky. Two children are sheltering in a hut amid the garbage, chatting as they sort among the items.

This lunar landscape overhangs Kigali. In the distance, the international airport, and all around, a necklace of a thousand hills.

On this island of garbage, there are well-established rules. There are leaders, deputies, a whole rigid hierarchy. The highest ranking get first pick, choosing the best finds: nails, tins, tiles, empty bottles, boxes, jerry cans.

At the end of the morning, buyers climb up the hill to the dump and come to assess the booty, to haggle, to buy. If they do not find buyers on the spot, some of the children go and sell their goods somewhere in town. Hunger, disease, violence, drugs go with them.

When they are too tired to go back and rummage in the dump, they take to stealing.

Children of the genocide, they are the wound that might kill the country all over again, for their suffering is bitter and their future extends no further than the end of the street. They will grow up with rage in their hearts for, after all, what does belonging matter? Life is cheap, life has no great value. Dying is no big deal, for death comes on the side of the road, in the dust or the mud. Those who come to give them weapons and enrol them in a barefoot army will know how to persuade them to fill the void of their wandering days. They are the open wound of memory, the suppurating sore.

THE YOUNG ZAÏREAN WOMAN WHO LOOKED LIKE A TUTSI

She is sitting on the edge of the divan. With her coppery skin, her high cheekbones and her sad smile, she is speaking in a voice so soft that you have to strain to hear her. She speaks very fast, not wanting to stop. The words come out of her mouth stripped of lies, of embellishment. In fact, she is lost in another world as she relives those terrible events. She's a girl like many others, not very educated, with no great ambition, who has been caught in the mesh of a murderous madness.

'It was evening, I'd finished eating and I was at home flicking through a magazine with my baby beside me. I heard rifle fire, but it didn't bother me because hereabouts you do hear gunshots from time to time. I told the houseboy to lock up and go to bed and then I put the baby in our bed because Etienne hadn't come home yet and I don't like to sleep alone, and also the baby's always waking me up during the night.

'Towards one o'clock in the morning, I awoke because of the sound of lots of gunfire. Etienne still wasn't back but I wasn't frightened, I wasn't at all bothered and went back to sleep. At six o'clock, the boy banged loudly on the bedroom door, the baby began to cry and I saw that Etienne still wasn't back which really surprised me, so I said: "What's the matter?" The boy shouted: "Madame, you must come quick, the Hutu soldiers are killing all the Tutsis!" Just then some soldiers passed the house and then one stops and he asks the boy who's run up to guard the door: "Is there anyone in the house?" "They all left ages ago," he replies. "And what if I go inside and find someone there?" The boy says again: "You can go in if you want." "If I find someone inside, I'll kill you along with them," shouts the soldier, so the boy says yes, and there I am hiding in the bathroom and I keep my hand over my child's mouth, for I was beginning to shake, but the soldier left saying he'd be back soon. Then the boy came to find me in a hurry, he said, "You look too much like a Tutsi, you must go quickly or they'll kill you, it's dangerous for you here, they know this area well."

'I wanted to run but in front of the house there is a man shouting: "Please, I beg you, don't shoot!" He puts his hands in the air and the soldier says: "You think I'm going to waste my bullets on you?" And then he takes his knife and he cuts his throat like a sheep, in front of the house where there are too many bodies, and I recognise some among them, they all used to live near the guy who was shouting, there's the man who sells vegetables in our area, and then there's another, the young mechanic who works at the end of the street and who fixes all the cars. I run with my child, terrified by the bodies I see on the way, I get to my Hutu neighbour's house but my head is spinning. She tells me to get inside quick and I spent my whole time there hiding under the bed with my child, there was also a Tutsi woman with her three children and her cousin.

'The third day, the neighbour said we must all leave her house because there are too many soldiers, I began to cry, you want us all to be killed if we go? I can't leave, we're all going to die here together. There was a lot of rifle fire, there was no way out, we stayed another two days and then the soldiers came into the yard of the house, they were breaking down all the doors to look for the Tutsis hiding there, I was sure I was going to die, I had to stay under the bed with my child.

'But they were already finding the others, I could see their feet and then I could hear shouting and then they sent everyone outside, and I could hear them talking a lot and sounding very angry. The neighbour was trying to apologise to them but all they do is shout: "Is there still anyone else here? If you don't tell us we'll kill you here and now, are there any Tutsis in the house?" And then they came back inside the house and started kicking all over the place and broke everything and took things and I was beginning to tremble too much, my baby cried, and they came and hauled me out from under the bed.

'I lost my head: "Why are you trembling like that? What are you hiding?" I said: "I'm not a Tutsi, I'm Zaïrean," and one of them hits me: "If you're Zaïrean why are you hiding? Tell me the truth or I'll kill you right now, give me your kid!" He put his pistol to my face and he lifted up the baby, I screamed, they killed my baby right there in front of me and then threw him into the yard, and I collapsed.

'When I woke up, it was dark, my vagina was sore and my dress was torn, I wept, there was no one left in the house, no light, I cried a lot, I heard rifle fire everywhere and I was trembling, I don't know how long I stayed like that, I crawled into the yard and I found my child's body, with my hands I dug a deepish hole and I put him in it and then I went back inside and wept some more in the house. I cried, I slept, I cried.

'I found a bit of food and every day I tried to go out, but I was too frightened they would find me and kill me. I found a good spot to hide in the roof of the house, whenever I heard a noise. One day, the soldiers came back and broke everything again, they shouted and they took away a whole lot of food. When I went back down, I saw that I was going to die because there was not enough food left, I was so disheartened, I didn't even have the strength to cry any more, if they want to kill me I don't care. I lay on the ground with my aching body and my skin covered with sores.

'Then when I heard some men coming into the house I realised that my suffering was going to come to an end since I knew they're going to find me and they're bound to kill me. They caught me, I got up, but I couldn't even look at them, are you alone here? Hurry up, come with us, don't shake like that, we're not going to kill you, we're RPF soldiers, I said: I'm not frightened but I want to go home to Zaïre because I'm a Zaïrean, they said: No point in talking.

'When they gathered us up to walk, there were lots of women, children and men all mixed up, there were lots of people who were crying, and children screaming, I saw a man I knew; he spoke to me and gave me lots of advice, he said he'd seen Etienne's body on that first day near a barrier in the district, when I heard that, my tears came back, then afterwards I found Léonie who lives behind our house, she explained to me how she'd run away and how she'd seen lots of dead people, I was distraught, I couldn't move, I was too sad, I say to Léonie with all those dead people I can see it's better if she goes on ahead, I'll follow on and she asks me why, I say no reason, I'm coming later, I've got to rest. She went on walking with the others.

'I stayed there sitting on the side of the road, I'm trying to work out how to kill myself, I want to take my scarf to pull it tight round my neck and then a soldier from the RPF comes along, he asks me why I'm sitting on the side of the road when people are leaving and I say: "I'm too tired, I want to die, I've already suffered enough because of the things I'm seeing and because of my child and my husband." He says: "You want to die? Don't you have a mother and father? Who's going to take care of them?" I begin to cry when I think of my mother and father who are in Zaïre, he says: "You've got this far so you can't die now," then he asked a woman who was passing to take me along with the others.

'On the road there were bodies everywhere and lots of men were dying, when the soldiers caught enemies, they took them behind us and you heard shots, on the road there were bodies everywhere, men and women and children too, but I never trod on a body, not even when the soldiers kept shouting: "Move forward!"

'At night we slept at the roadside, one evening I dreamt that a corpse told me that the house he had left in Kigali was for his son and the car for his brother, I was frightened but I said: "You haven't even got arms or feet or a mouth and you're speaking this way?" He said to me: "Are you making fun of me? You've been lucky, you're not dead." And then I saw how he was getting up to catch me, and I screamed loudly and Léonie next to me, she touched me and she said: "What's the matter?" I told her the dream and then in the morning we went on our way and after a few days we stopped at a camp. The others stayed there, but I went off to Zaïre in a lorry.

'Back home with my parents, they gave me a lot of sympathy, I sleep in the same bed as my mum, and she holds me tight in her arms to help me to sleep, I told her I want to go back to bury my baby properly, at night I am always afraid, I dream of the child's corpse swollen like a pig on the road and all his clothes were torn but still he looked at me, even today I can't forget that body, even now I can't be alone in a house, if someone knocks on the door, I have to listen quickly and stop what I'm doing because I'm so frightened by everything I've seen.'

TRAVELLING COURT MARTIAL AT NTONGWE

Military tribunal. Trial of Edouard Mujyambere, sub-lieutenant in the former government army

17 June 1999: first hearing. Judgement deferred.
20 July 1999: second hearing.

◆

The prisoner wipes his hands against each other. He meticulously picks fluff off his body, his clothes. He's wearing a green short-sleeved shirt and shorts, nicely ironed – the uniform of military prisoners. He has plastic sandals. He is young. His hair has been cut recently. In front of him, on a small table, he has placed his papers, neatly arranged in a file which he is constantly opening and shutting. You can see his neat writing, a bit like a homework essay. He rubs his hands at regular intervals and cracks his finger joints. It is a strange sound in this courtroom where everything is quiet. Everyone sits down for the hearing. The judge has asked the witnesses to leave the room. The villagers are there, sitting on benches. They are waiting. Soldiers are guarding the door. The room is well ventilated. It is cool after the heat and the dust of outside. A crow, perched on one of the big trees that overhang the building, caws in distress.

The prisoner is seated opposite the judge. He turns around occasionally looking for a face among those present. I have the impression that I know him, that I have seen him at home, in one of the streets of the capital.

The attorney for the defence begins. He underlines the fact

that the accused was arrested in 1995. Since then, other accusations of genocide have been added to the charges against him. He was denounced and verbally accused of complicity with a major who is in jail in Tanzania. But since no formal proof has yet been provided, he asks that the trial continue without taking these new charges into account. The first hearing had already been deferred for similar reasons.

In his reply, the public prosecutor nevertheless demands a further delay so as to be able to gather the necessary documents for the new grounds for accusation. A period of eight weeks would allow him to seek the major's extradition from Tanzania.

The defence retorts that the extradition process is long and uncertain: 'After four years of detention, we must now consider the current charges.'

Now it's the accused's turn to speak. He pleads not guilty. He explains how he was arrested. He holds his file in his hands while he talks. He explains, goes on explaining . . . He says it's all a conspiracy against him, that these are false testimonies so as to take his father's house from him, after his father died during the war. People are also trying to take his field from him.

Yes, he fought against the RPF at Byumba and Kigali and when the soldiers finally took the capital, he fled like everyone else. He sought refuge in Goma, in Zaïre. But when the new president asked all those who had done nothing wrong to come home, he came back and rejoined the army. He also went back to his old neighbourhood to take possession of the family home. That was when all this business began, he states. A year after rejoining the army, he was arrested. Yet, for another two months, his salary was paid.

The judges look at each other. They are wearing dark green uniforms, made of a thick material. They have stripes on their shoulders.

The court retires.

Everyone waits. The defence attorney speaks to the prisoner. On the other side of the room, the public prosecutor is all alone. Some peasants approach him to seek damages and interest in relation to the case in progress. He writes down in a big book what is being whispered in his ear. People are speaking in low voices.

The prisoner recognises a girl among those present. They go up to one another and by his way of expressing himself you can see he is giving her instructions. Those close by are watching them wide-eyed.

The court resumes. Everyone rises.

Hearing adjourned to 24 August 1999 at 10 a.m.

THE PASTOR

Some desperate parents who were fleeing had entrusted their four children to a pastor to look after them at his home and protect them. But very shortly afterwards, militiamen arrived and ransacked the house. When they found the children, they killed them.

The pastor is now accused of having himself called the militia and of having killed at least one of the children with his own hands. An old woman says in his defence: 'His house was completely ransacked, how could he have been a party to that?'

But the pastor pleads guilty. He confirms that he had indeed taken responsibility for the children. When the militia came to his house, they forced him to kill one of the children with his own hands. He says he struck one blow of the machete. When he saw the blood flowing, he fled. He was on the run in the bush for a long time. Then he managed to join a refugee camp.

At the end of the war, he surrendered himself voluntarily to justice.

He asks for forgiveness. He killed in spite of himself. 'I have settled my account with God. I have sought His forgiveness. It is for you humans now to decide what you are going to do with me.'

When the prosecutor asked him if he knew what his punishment should be, he replied: 'I must die.'

RILISSA PRISON

Seven thousand prisoners

From the track, you can see the lake which casts its silvery reflections on to the dry, reddish-brown savannah. Sorghum fields mark the prison grounds. A prisoner is standing in the middle of a field. His job is to scare away the birds.

Near the administration buildings, in a sort of a field, sorghum stalks are slowly burning. An acrid smell assails your nostrils.

In the gloom of a small office, a prisoner is kneeling before the lawyer who has come to take his deposition and draw up his case file. Seated at a small table, the lawyer is listening to the man. On his face, an expression of weariness. He has heard the same words a thousand times before. The prisoner is pleading not guilty.

On the wall a blackboard lists the categories of prisoners: 'Pleaded guilty. Found guilty. Condemned to death. Without files. Women. Sick'.

In this model prison, a foreign organisation is proposing a programme of reforms. They suggest occupying the prisoners with agricultural work, fish farming, and raising stock. Hundreds of prisoners in their sugar-pink uniform are tilling the fields and tending the vegetable gardens. Green shoots create abstract art on the black earth. Water buckets for irrigation. Hoes, machetes. Peasant farmers return to being peasant farmers, rediscovering forgotten gestures, the breathing of the earth. Only one or two guards. Everything is peaceful, almost beautiful under an intensely blue sky. The regularity of the furrows suggests there will be good crops.

As night falls, the men march in single file back to the prison. The lake prepares for the night. In the growing darkness, the pink trail of their uniforms snakes through the tall grass.

They say there are very few suicides in the prisons, but apparently there are guards who kill themselves. One day, one of them came home, and in the dead of night got up without saying anything to his wife. He took his rifle and shot himself in the head.

Or this former RPF soldier, who had become a prison guard, who went mad when he heard that the Gacaca was going to begin. He went into the prison, shot four prisoners and then turned the weapon on himself.

The Gacaca means a return to traditional justice. How did the ancestors judge? How did they mete out punishment? Traditional customs are being revived in the face of this emergency. Solutions for the present must be sought in the past. If official justice is to be relied on, it would take over a hundred years to hear the cases of all the prisoners. The aim: to open one area of justice to the people, to give back to the citizens the privilege of passing judgement.

To give back to communities their spirit of independence.

But who will be the judge and who will be the accused? The survivors are a minority. How can they bear witness to the cruelty that has been inflicted upon them as well as the suffering of those who are dead?

Did the ancestors know the crime of genocide?

◆

97

What is to be done with this mass of people, these thousands of prisoners in a single space, every centimetre of ground occupied, like in an overcrowded market? How are they to be fed, clothed, looked after, kept occupied? How can this potentially explosive energy be channelled?

Cell blocks for those pleading guilty, for those who have not yet pleaded guilty, for those who have been sentenced, for those sentenced to death or to life imprisonment.

There aren't enough guards, not enough of anything.

Not enough food, not enough staple food in particular. Not enough water. The prisoners fetch it from the lake.

Not enough doctors, medicine, space. Waiting in the entrance of a common cell, separated from the other prisoners by mere centimetres, the sick await an unlikely cure. AIDS lurks among the crowd. Dysentery. Tuberculosis. And when they die, they are buried, over there, behind the prison walls.

The whole of society is represented here: former politicians, businessmen, civil servants, managers, teachers, artists, school-children, students, peasant farmers, doctors, women, priests, pastors, nuns . . .

The prisoners police themselves. How could it be otherwise? They have established a hierarchy, given themselves titles they've created themselves such as 'capitan', 'vice-capitan', set up categories such as 'disciplinary section', 'gate security', 'water safety', 'building security', 'kitchen section', 'hairdressing security'. Rank, authority, the old scheme of things is being set up again. The agronomist supervises the work in the fields, the nurse supervises medical care, the teacher explains things. What have they talked about all these years? And what if they have already taken their future into their own hands? They know that their number is a force, a power greater than their imprisonment.

The prisoners pray morning and evening, each religion in turn, the Catholics, then the Protestants, the Muslims and all the various sects. Among them, there are some pastors who officiate. Some of the prisoners wear rosaries round their necks. The pastor has made his confession. He confessed so as to provide an example for the Christians. He killed three people whom he did not know. The Rwandan people have seen a lot of violence, he says. But those who have fled the country have broken the chain of memory since they are not there to help the prisoners to reconstruct the events.

◆

Wednesday and Saturday, visiting days.

A line of prisoners stands opposite a line of visitors. There is a distance of several metres separating them. They shout words at each other.

SECTION FOR THOSE CONDEMNED TO DEATH OR LIFE IMPRISONMENT

Eighty-five men in a room with a small courtyard. They are not allowed out. When they see us arrive, one of them says immediately: 'All we can see is a bit of sky and the door to this courtyard. No books. Nothing to write on. Bibles, occasionally. One prisoner cannot testify in another's defence. Only those who survived the genocide can testify. It's a betrayal created between the courts and the genocide survivors. And what about those who have killed, but have also saved lives? The courts should take that into account. Why is there no follow-up when someone appeals? Where are the copies of the judgements? Why don't we ever get visits from humanitarian organisations? Some people have pleaded guilty, so why have they still been condemned to death? What should be punished is false testimony, false accusations.

'The witnesses for the prosecution are living in our houses and taking our possessions. The judges are among the genocide survivors. How can they judge our cases impartially?

'Who will punish the war crimes committed during the liberation? The murders carried out in reprisal? And all those people who took part in the massacres before the genocide of 1994, are they going to be punished as well?

'We need to get angry with the political classes. They're living in exile. And when some high-ranking official is arrested, at the international court of Arusha, there's no death penalty. It's only the little folk who are executed.'

The man speaking in the name of those condemned to death looks like the man in the street. Nothing about him suggests guilt. What you notice most is his intelligence, his level of education. He knows that time is ticking away, so he needs to be persuasive.

'Write it down,' he insists. 'Tell everybody. And if you can, send us some notebooks and pens to write with.'

SECTION 15

Two hundred and fifty-three women

A group of women. They are sitting in a circle at the end of the yard which is reserved for their use. On the other side of an invisible line, men are singing and dancing to the sound of drums. Whistle blasts beat the time. One after another, several youths jump and spin round.

Some children cross freely between the two territories.

Several of the women are singing too. What do the words mean? 'They are "songs of God",' explains the 'capitan'.

Another group is doing basketwork in silence. Close by, a

100

handful of women are praying aloud, hands raised heavenwards, heads thrown back, eyes closed.

The children came with their mothers when they were too young to be separated from them. They will leave the prison when they are about three years old. They go out every morning accompanied by a female prisoner, a former primary school teacher. One woman was pregnant when she arrived. Her baby is eighteen months old.

Where do they sleep at night? In their building, stretched out side by side.

They are divided by age groups: mothers, girls, mature women, the old. One room is kept for the sick.

Do women become pregnant during their detention? 'Yes,' replies the capitan, 'but that was before, when there was corruption. That's finished now that the new director is here. The old one made the prisoners build houses for him out of the money from the budget.'

There are few visits. It is other women who come to see them: daughters, aunts, cousins, mothers. The husbands and sons are in exile, dead or in jail. They get fruit, food, clothes. The baskets they make are gifts they give to their visitors. To sell them?

Women who are murderers, perpetrators of genocide, women forced to kill, accused of having killed their husbands, their children, friends, neighbours, strangers. Women who have helped men to rape, who sang to give them the courage to massacre, who betrayed, who pillaged, who decided to join in the acts of cruelty. With machetes, they killed other women, mutilated children, finished off men. They joined with the militia and armed peasant farmers to surround the places where those trying to flee had taken refuge. They went into hospitals, churches, schools to take part in the slaughter. They took money from the dead, jewellery from dead women, their clothes. Most of the victims of the massacres were stripped, left completely naked.

◆

Sometimes, even, at night, a mother would drag her children along to the homes of the victims to ransack them and strip the corpses to take everything of value from them. Others roamed the neighbourhoods accompanied by their murdering sons.

Educated women, agitators, officials, accusers, organisers. These women killed their own destiny as women. How many of them are now in flight? Where are they hiding? In the towns? In the hills? On the country's borders?

We would have preferred them to be innocent.

We can shut our eyes to the ugliness of the world. But we must open our pupils to see the truth. 'Don't be frightened of knowing,' says a female genocide survivor.

Only impunity gives birth to death.

FRODUARD, THE YOUNG FARMER TURNED MURDERER

'Running down the hills singing, you had to be quick, you had to strike without really knowing what you were doing, do it all at once; cut, strike with a machete, a club, a metal bar, a pickaxe. You would strike a blow, and sometimes you wouldn't even take the time to watch the blood flow, quickly, the fractured skull, the screams that don't reach your ears, only the sound of gunfire close by and the stench of death which would intoxicate all your senses and engulf all that had been part of your life before. There'd be someone cutting off an arm, and you'd be striking out where you could and others would just be watching you and you had to prove that you could kill, and it was so easy: a life isn't very strong, it's not solid, you strike a blow and a hand falls off, another and the skull splits. They gave us clubs and told us where to strike: it was them or us and there was no greater fear than that, that they were the ones wanting to kill us, who would one day kill us if any of them survived. We had to work fast because time was what was going to win the victory. If we wanted to do it, we just had to go ahead and do it, because there was no going back. If we lost the war we would all die. Some kept asking for mercy. What mercy? They wanted to die by the gun instead of the machete, but that would have cost more, because mercy is expensive. Would they have shown us any mercy? They would have massacred the lot of us. The doors were broken down and soldiers were lobbing grenades where they were hiding and then we went in to finish off the job and the ones who still wouldn't die, we took them outside to kill them and make sure they were properly dead, even if we had to chop them into little pieces, and there were people there who were capable of doing that. I saw an old woman kill her neighbour's child with a studded stick, and when she said, "We don't need to bother about the other kids," she was killed by a militiaman along with all the children of the other woman. You couldn't afford to hesitate, you had to obey orders and get on with the job. One day we went with the soldiers to a businessman's yard. He had a Peugeot and a truck. The soldiers went into his house and fired some shots bang, bang, bang! And they killed him with his wife and three children. Then they took the vehicles and drove off. Then we were able to go in and take the TV, the radio and everything we could find in the house. That's how we were able to go to someone's house when we knew they had got rich by exploiting the Hutus and had pillaged the country like the members of the royal family in the olden days.

When we arrived in a district, we'd get together to surround them like when you're hunting, we'd shout and bang on the windows, the doors, we'd throw stones on the roofs and there were some people who were so terrified that they'd run out to try and escape and we'd catch them easily, and then there were others who tried to hide, but we knew all their little hiding places, under beds, in the toilets, in the ceiling, outside, in the undergrowth, in ditches, in gutters, we knew all the places to flush them out of, or catch them. We didn't only wound them, we were supposed to kill them once and for all. We were carrying out a programme. So we wanted to succeed in our operation. We did the bulk of the work and it was up to the soldiers to finish it off. When the president was alive, he had said that we needed to get rid of traitors who had left the country for weapons training. And then when the president died, we were told that the Tutsis had killed him but that if they wanted to come here, they wouldn't find any of their accomplices still alive. They wouldn't find anyone to help them kill the Hutus. We had to strike back, defend ourselves. We had to scupper the Tutsi conspiracy. We also had to get rid of the Hutus who talked like Tutsis, RPF-lovers. In meetings the advisers would say, "Either you kill them or they will kill you." It was easy because we all knew the list of people to kill in the targeted areas. In the hills everyone knows everyone else, you couldn't hide your identity. Every night, when we were locating the accomplices, the enemy, the orders would come to the road blocks and when they tried to pass to run away with their families, they'd be discovered and killed on the spot. We had to kill them all because if any of them escaped, they could go and join the RPF army rebels and come back and attack us. We had to kill the children too, because many of the RPF leaders were children themselves when they fled the country. The cleansing had to be absolutely total. On the radio, we heard that the grave wasn't yet full, that we had to help to fill it. They told us: "If you're not sure if it's a Tutsi, all you have to do is look at him, his size, his face, you just have to look at his delicate little nose and break it. To finish the job, take your machetes, take your spears, get yourselves some support from the soldiers. You've got to exterminate the RPF agents because they are accursed." In my head I can still hear the words of the presenter. "Fight! Crush them! Up and at 'em! With your spears, your sticks, your rifles, your swords, stones, run them through, these cockroaches, these enemies of democracy, show you know how to defend yourselves, give your soldiers some encouragement. If you are a farmer and you hear shots, stop your work and go and fight. You've got to be a farmer and a soldier at the same time!"

'Yes, there was absolutely no doubt, the enemy had to disappear from our country. They thought they could gather strength again and return to occupy Rwanda but thanks to our weapons, we were able to kill them. We had to search every area, every hill, every neighbourhood and that's what we did.'

JOSÉPHINE

Joséphine did not want to tell me whether she was a Hutu or a Tutsi. I was ashamed of having asked her.

She has an adolescent daughter, Philomène, and Gratien, a boy of six. She is also raising several orphan nieces. She shakes her head, looking worried: 'I've got problems with my daughter. I'm always quarrelling with her because she's so stubborn. She'll never say she's sorry. When she fights with her little brother, he always has to make the first move. Even if she's in the wrong, she won't apologise. He, on the other hand, is always quick to make it up. Everyone knows how hard-hearted Philomène is. I keep telling her how important it is to be able to say you're sorry. If she can't do it herself, who will do it for her? I'm making a big deal of it because I really think it is very important. I don't know how often I've punished her for this.

'When we were in the house during the troubles, we used to spend all day praying. The children were frightened but they didn't say anything. They never complained.

'We never really knew what was going on outside. We only heard gunfire and screams. Twice, the soldiers came here. The first time, it was to ask us how many people were in the house. When I told them, they left. The second time, they made us go outside and they went and searched inside. But one of them said they had too much to do and they didn't stay long. We stayed indoors for a few days. When there was some noise in the courtyard and we saw armed men through the window, I told my children: "I think we're going to die today. Whatever happens, pray and be brave." The children replied: "Yes, Mother," and we went outside.

'They were RPF soldiers. They took us with several other families to Byumba. We walked all the way there in a kind of procession. There were lots of people, women and children mostly.'

And your husband?

'He wasn't with us. A few days before the genocide began, he'd left on a business trip. My sister wasn't with us either.'

Where is he now?

'He never came back. I found my sister again at the end of the war.

'Our neighbourhood was never really badly affected because the RPF took control of it right at the start. I never witnessed any horrible slaughter. In the streets I saw the results of these massacres, but I was never actually present when they happened.

'In the camp the children did nothing. I didn't let my daughter go and get wood because it was too dangerous for her to go any distance. She could have been kidnapped or raped in the bush. The children amused themselves any way they could. We lived without news of our friends and relatives.

'When we finally went home in July, we went back to our house. It was badly damaged. The neighbourhood was deserted. Everywhere there were ruins, debris, broken objects scattered about, filth, dirt, stones. The stench of death was terrible, unbearable. We had come back to a ruined land.

'We lived in one room for several months. Gradually, we rebuilt. The government gave me a few sheets of corrugated iron. Even now, when I have a bit of money, it goes into the rebuilding.

'If I were to say anything to the children about war, I would make them realise that it came from hatred and being over-ambitious. It's all very well to be ambitious, but you've got to be realistic too. You mustn't want too much. You've got to be happy with what you can get by honest means. And above all, you must never believe politicians. They don't tell the truth. They've only got their own interests at heart. They made a huge number of people believe that the genocide was in their interest. They told the peasant farmers they could take lots of things, that they would be rich. In a small country, land is scarce and the plots are getting smaller and smaller. They told them they could take the land, the cattle. They encouraged them to do evil things while they were busy looking after their own interests. Now, they've almost all gone, taking their money with them. They're living quietly somewhere, while the poor people are suffering every day. They are locked up in overcrowded prisons or, worse, in municipal cells set up in former offices or schools. They're not given any food there. Their families have to provide food for them. The women can't work any more. They've got to spend their time looking for food. They've got no one to help

107

them till the fields. The children don't go to school any more. Trials are long and the peasant farmers don't really understand the procedure, or the consequences of the verdicts.

'Luckily, in towns like Butare, the population wasn't so easily persuaded. But they managed to get to the very basis of the community, right down to the simple peasant farmers, by invoking the authority of the traditional hierarchical structure. They gave them money, weapons, alcohol and the radio, and by use of slogans and words of hatred, encouraged them to kill.

'No, it wasn't an ethnic war, because at the highest level they got together to pillage the country, to look after their own interests. Politicians never tell the truth. They stir up hatred. When the country is poor and the youth are unemployed, they can easily manipulate people by making others the cause of their troubles.

'Today what matters to me is not to be frightened any more for my kids, for my family. To live in peace because Rwanda is my country, my homeland.

'The hardest thing is when we think of all those who have died that we'll never see again. It's hard even if you haven't lost anyone because it's a collective grief which will probably stay with us all our lives.

'But perhaps our children will be able to live in freedom, without fear. They, perhaps, will be able to live again.'

THE SEVEN WONDERS

'We were seven friends on campus. We'd been nicknamed "the Seven Wonders" because it was wonderful to see us together. We did everything alike. We went to lectures in the same lecture theatres, played the same sports, were in the same football or volleyball teams. Of course, we were often more than seven because we had our girlfriends with us. The campus belonged to us. There were problems, naturally, but what interested us was to live our lives like all young people.

'It was towards 1990 that I really became aware of the division between the Hutus, the Tutsis and the Twas. Before, I hadn't really taken much notice. My mother was a Tutsi and my father a Hutu. My parents sometimes spoke of what had happened in 1959, when the King died and then some massacres took place, but they had never properly explained about the ethnic divide. Now, I believe that it was a taboo subject for them. We chose our friends as we liked and no one ever made any critical comment about that. I had never asked my friends what ethnic group they belonged to. We spoke the same language, we had the same names, we had the same concerns, what would have been the point?

'Yet, deep down, we knew that our relatives were divided by ethnic hatred and the propaganda of Hutu Power. On campus, we all knew who were the partisan lecturers and who were those against. The "Ten Commandments of the Hutus" were known to everyone, but as far as we knew, only a few hotheads were bothered about them. For our part, we tried to be above all that, not take any notice of that filth.

'When the president's plane crashed in Kigali on 6 April, the killing did not begin right away where we were. As time passed, we heard that soldiers and militia were going into public places and targeting people who were known for their progressive ideas. Lecturers disappeared from their homes and a few days later we would hear that they had been seen in the back of a truck full of soldiers. We began to be really frightened, especially when the news from Kigali was very bad and the prefect of the town, who had tried to restore order, was summarily replaced. I hid at Jean-Jacques's place. I had no news of my parents. I stayed in his room during all the troubles. He fed me, went out secretly to get me food. From the window, I could sometimes see what was going on outside. I saw a group of militiamen go inside a house, firing as they went. There was a teacher living there with his family. They forced them outside and shot them in the garden. I was lucky, I was never found.

'My parents want me to go back to my studies now, but I don't want to. I prefer to work and save to go and study in another country. The university is full of former soldiers who fought for liberation and who think like soldiers. They look down on us. Am I a Hutu? Am I a Tutsi? Everyone asks me where I was during the genocide and how I managed to keep safe. Yet everyone knows what happened. There are only four left of our group. Damien and Valens are dead. Jean de Dieu has fled the country. People know what he did. He was seen in the hills with the militia. Others say that he manned a barricade.

'Gallican and Patrice aren't doing anything. Gallican lost a leg. I haven't seen them for a long time. Jean-Jacques is the one I see most often, even though not very frequently because he is very busy. He also wants to leave but as he lost his father and his older brother, he has to help his mother take care of his younger brothers and sisters. He says he's waiting for them to grow up so that he can leave.

'As for me, the future consists of one day just following another. How can you envisage the future here? What future? Tomorrow seems a long way off to me. Plan what? So much can happen so quickly. From one day to the next, you have to begin all over again. When the war ended, we thought that everything could at last go back to normal, that we could start again on a better foundation. Not make the same mistakes again. But after a few years, everything seems to be settling back into place: corruption, impunity, uncertainty. Promises are not kept. They vanish one after another. Reconciliation? We need justice! To know that those who should be punished will be

110

punished. But things drag on. It seems as though nothing is moving forward, that gradually everything is falling into oblivion. No one wants to be weighed down by that unbearable memory. Those who survived are there to remind us of the past and we would prefer them not to be in the forefront any more so that the country can rebuild itself more quickly, so that money will come back. The survivors are an embarrassment, the prisoners are an embarrassment. We want to freeze our memories in monuments of stone.

'There is not enough work. There is no money in the country. Mutual aid has become difficult. No one trusts anyone else. Everyone takes refuge in themselves. How can we build something together, sit at the same table?

'I would like to go and live in Canada. I've got a cousin living there. Or perhaps in Britain. Is it difficult to register at a university?'

HUTU POWER:

The Ten Commandments of the Hutus

1 Every Hutu man must know that a Tutsi woman, wherever she may be, works in the interest of her Tutsi ethnic group. Consequently we consider a traitor any Hutu man who:

- marries a Tutsi woman,
- becomes friendly with a Tutsi woman,
- employs a Tutsi woman as a secretary or mistress.

2 Every Hutu must recognise that our Hutu girls are better and more conscientious in their roles of woman, wife and mother. Are they not beautiful, good secretaries and more honest?

3 Hutu women, be vigilant and try to bring your husbands, brothers and sons to do what is right.

4 Every Hutu man must understand that all Tutsis are dishonest when it comes to business matters. Their only aim is to achieve the supremacy of their ethnic group. Consequently, any Hutu is to be considered a traitor who does any of the following:

- doing business with a Tutsi,
- investing his own or government money in a Tutsi enterprise,
- lending money to or borrowing money from Tutsis,

- rendering any kind of service to a Tutsi in business (obtaining of an import licence, bank credits, site construction, public contracts . . .).

5 All strategic positions, be they political, administrative, economic, military or security, must be given to Hutus.

6 Hutus must be in the majority in the education sector (school pupils, students, teachers).

7 The Rwandan armed forces must be exclusively Hutu. The experience of the October War (1990) taught us a lesson. No member of the army may marry a Tutsi woman.

8 The Hutus must stop feeling sorry for the Tutsis.

9 The Hutus, wherever they are, must show unity and solidarity and must feel concern for the fate of their Hutu brothers.

- Hutus inside and outside Rwanda must be constantly on the lookout for friends and allies who support the Hutu cause, beginning with their Bantu brothers.
- They must constantly fight against Tutsi propaganda.
- Hutus must stand firm and be vigilant towards their common enemy, the Tutsis.

10 The social revolution of 1959, the referendum of 1961 and the Hutu ideology must be taught to all Hutus at every level. Everyone must widely propagate this ideology. Every Hutu who persecutes his Hutu brother for having read, passed on or taught this ideology is himself a traitor.

(Published in the pro-Hutu extremists' journal *Kangura*, 10 December 1990.)

CAMP KIBEHO, SOUTH-WEST RWANDA

22 April 1995

When the first shots were heard inside the camp at Kibeho, the Hutu refugees, knowing they were surrounded by government forces, had turned on each other with machetes. These were probably clashes between those wanting to leave and those wanting to stay. It also seems likely that torrential rain caused a sudden movement from the crowd that made the soldiers fire. What is certain is that the shots into the crowd created such panic that a stampede ensued in which many people were trampled underfoot, mostly women and children. Grenades were thrown and the army fired mortars. The soldiers also fired on those who were trying to flee.

The observers who arrived after the attack was over later counted between five and eight thousand dead and hundreds of wounded.

Kibeho, with its population of over eighty thousand refugees, was one of the biggest camps set up in the region. Hundreds of thousands of Hutus had fled their villages after the genocide for fear of reprisals.

The new government in power since the liberation was anxious to demonstrate its determination to get rid of the sprawling refugee camps where former genocidal militiamen mingled with the civilian population and were re-creating the hierarchy and the chains of command that had made it possible to organise the genocide of almost a million Tutsis and moderate Hutus. Protected and fed by the humanitarian organisations, they were getting ready to re-arm.

After the carnage of Kibeho, some two hundred and fifty thousand Hutus in the surrounding area were forced to return home.

◆

History was going into reverse. The executioners were becoming the victims, the victims the executioners.

As if violence would never cease to engender violence.

SISTER AGATHA

'For from within, out of the heart of man, come evil thoughts . . .' Mark, VII, 21

'Evil has always existed at the heart's core. It is the fire of moral decay burning dully like eternally glowing embers. It is the moral decay of a human being devouring his own kind, devouring his own flesh.

'Listen to this tale of a monster which was always hungry:

'Every day, the villagers brought food, huge quantities of food, to a monster which swallowed everything, though he was never satisfied. In desperation, they gathered together all the resources of the world and gave them to him. He ate them.

'He devoured the earth, the sun, the moon, the stars, but he was still hungry.

'Then, as nothing remained, neither in the heavens nor on the earth, he looked at his hand. He thought it huge, plump and appetising. He ate one of his fingers, then two, then three and so on. He crunched up his right hand. He crunched up

115

his left hand, his arms, both his shoulders. But still he was hungry.

'In the end, he consumed himself altogether.

◆

'The concept of Evil existed even before the first sparks of sunlight, before the earth and the sky came together, and before the waters gave birth to the enormous womb of the oceans.

'Evil existed long before the breath of life, long before the presence of gods on earth.

'Good, its inseparable brother, was there too, its vulnerable alter ego, threatened by time and indifference.

'To disarm our urges for death, we must recognise within ourselves the fears that drive us. We must draw the sting from the wounds of the past, our own wounds and those that others have inflicted upon us, those we have inherited from our parents and those we might pass on to our children. The wounds buried deep in our hearts.

'We must lay down arms and let the wounds heal and scar over.

'Blood has a sweet flavour. Like the bees which buzz around the hive overflowing with honey, he who accepts Evil with complete impunity will make a royal feast of it.

'Hatred lies dormant in us all. What most torments us is that unpredictable feeling in our hearts which can awaken and tip us into a parallel universe. Who knows what I might do tomorrow if the threat of punishment were removed? If I saw before me a vast unexplored territory where my previous humiliations, my frustrations could all be avenged? A world in which the laws of a past morality would suddenly vanish.

◆

116

'To erase all humanity. To look no more into the faces of others. Above all to exchange no more glances. An animal, a heap of flesh. A skull cracking like a dry branch.

'To drink enough alcohol to be released from all hesitation, and to wipe out all memory of daily life. To remain in ignorance of doubt so that the act is nothing more than a gesture of unbelievable power. To be master of the slave kneeling at one's feet. God made man.

◆

'But Good has not disappeared, has not been buried in the mass graves. We shall go on raising altars to our saints and our heroes. We shall go on marvelling at acts of goodness and bravery. In the terrible darkness, some men and women have raised themselves higher than the fate that should have been theirs.

'When the balm of time has healed our sorrows, and the generations can hold their heads up once more, the history of all those who succeeded in preserving their humanity will be told over and over again, recounted in whispered words, sung aloud, danced and celebrated.

'See how life resumes its course. Hear the voices of the dead who are now at peace and sleeping in the wind. They whisper to us that the time for all torment must cease and that they are ready to withdraw so that the living may take their places.

'Darkness has hidden the sunlight and shadow has engulfed the earth.

'We shall emerge from this long and terrifying eclipse.'

THE SECOND RETURN

I have not recovered from Rwanda. Rwanda cannot be exorcised. Danger is ever-present, lurking in the memory, crouching in the bush in neighbouring countries. Violence is still there, on every side.

Death and cruelty.

Death is natural. It is the other side of life and we should not be afraid of it. And if you want to come closer to Rwanda, you must put it aside. Besides, death is not stronger than life, for life always regains the upper hand in the end.

It is human violence that has made death cruel, hideous. An eternal monster in the memory of time.

We need to understand, to analyse the mechanisms of hatred, the words that create division, the deeds that put the seal on treason, the actions that unleash terror.

We need to understand. Our humanity is in peril.

Acknowledgments

This book forms part of a collective project entitled 'Rwanda: writing as a duty to memory' initiated by the Fest'Africa festival (African Arts and Media Association) and sponsored by the Fondation de France which, in the context of its 'Artists' Initiative' programme, in 1998 invited about ten African writers to take up a Writing Fellowship in Rwanda to reflect on the memory of the genocide that had taken place.

My gratitude goes to the authors of the various works on Rwanda for their huge contribution in endeavouring to make sense of and explain the genocide. I would also like to thank all those with whom I came into contact during my trip and who were willing to let me hear their voices.